THE TALENT
SUTRA

Also by Devdutt Pattanaik

The Leadership Sutra: An Indian Approach to Power
My Gita
The Success Sutra: An Indian Approach to Wealth
Business Sutra: A Very Indian Approach to Management

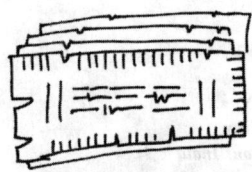

THE TALENT
SUTRA

AN INDIAN APPROACH TO LEARNING

DEVDUTT
PATTANAIK

Illustrated by the author

ALEPH BOOK COMPANY
An independent publishing firm
promoted by *Rupa Publications India*

First published in India in 2016
by Aleph Book Company
7/16 Ansari Road, Daryaganj
New Delhi 110 002

Copyright © Devdutt Pattanaik 2016

The author has asserted his moral rights.

All rights reserved.

The views and opinions expressed in this book are
the author's own and the facts are as reported by
him, which have been verified to the extent possible,
and the publishers are not in any way liable for the
same.

No part of this publication may be reproduced,
transmitted, or stored in a retrieval system, in any
form or by any means, without permission in
writing from Aleph Book Company.

ISBN: 978-93-83064-27-4

7 9 10 8 6

For sale in the Indian subcontinent only

Printed in India

This book is sold subject to the condition that it
shall not, by way of trade or otherwise, be lent,
resold, hired out, or otherwise circulated without the
publisher's prior consent in any form of binding or
cover other than that in which it is published.

Contents

Introduction ix

The Talent Sutra 1

Isolation 11

Reflection 33

Expansion 57

Inclusion 79

Conclusion 113
Notes 117
Index of Sutras 125

Introduction

Saraswati is the goddess of knowledge in Hinduism, as well as in Buddhism and Jainism. Her name is derived from fluidity (saras) of the imagination. Human imagination enables us to invent and innovate, visualize, plan and de-risk. Yet imagination is a bad word in the world of business and management. It strips us of certainty. We want to control the imagination of those who work for us, prevent their minds from wandering from work. Yet every human being lives in an imagined reality. Recognizing this enables us to work with talent, build strong relationships and nurture people to face any situation with faith and patience. Failure to recognize imagination is why family-owned businesses are unable to manage professionals and how professionally-run companies end up creating ineffective mechanistic talent management systems. Training, learning and development, are not just about skills and knowledge and competencies, they are about appreciating the human-animal,

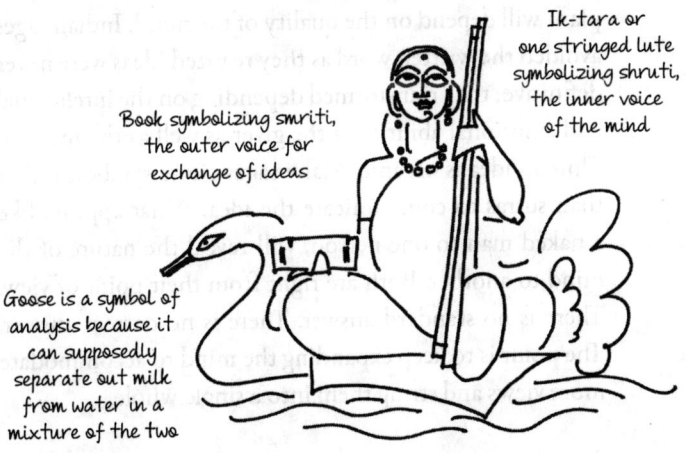

Book symbolizing smriti, the outer voice for exchange of ideas

Ik-tara or one stringed lute symbolizing shruti, the inner voice of the mind

Goose is a symbol of analysis because it can supposedly separate out milk from water in a mixture of the two

recognizing that neither we nor those around us are programmable machines that we can plug and play. Managing people, hence relationships, is key to the survival of an organization. Hence, *The Talent Sutra*, a work derived from my book on Indian approach to business and management, *Business Sutra*, focuses on sutras related to creativity in the workplace, nurturing talent and the importance of teamwork.

Ideas in this book are provided in the form of 'sutras'. Sutra (the word or concept) has two meanings:

- It means a string meant to join dots to create a pattern. The book strings together myriad ideas from Jain, Hindu and Buddhist traditions to create a synthesized whole that helps us understand the Indian way. Likewise it strings together Greek and biblical ideas to understand the Western way and Confucian and Taoist ideas to understand the Chinese way. Each one of these garlands are man-made and reveal my truth, not the truth.
- Sutra also means an aphorism, a terse statement. The book is full of these. They are like seeds which, when planted in the mind, germinates into a plant. The nature of the plant will depend on the quality of the mind. Indian sages avoided the written word as they realized ideas were never definitive; they transformed depending on the intellectual and emotional abilities of the giver as well as the receiver. Thus an idea is organic. Many sages chose symbols rather than sutras to communicate the idea. What appears like a naked man to one person, will reveal the nature of the mind to another. Both are right from their point of view. There is no standard answer. There is no correct answer. The point is to keep expanding the mind to accommodate more views and string them into a single whole.

These sutras are 'made in India' but are 'for the world', for they complement modern management by drawing attention back from profit, through hunger, to humanity.

THE TALENT SUTRA

Isolation *Reflection* *Expansion* *Inclusion*

The ability to see the human quest for identity is darshan. The identity of a person or sukshma-sharira is how he imagines himself. And this identity depends on brahmanda, how he imagines the world. Identity and worldview are thus manas putra, the children of Brahma's imagination.

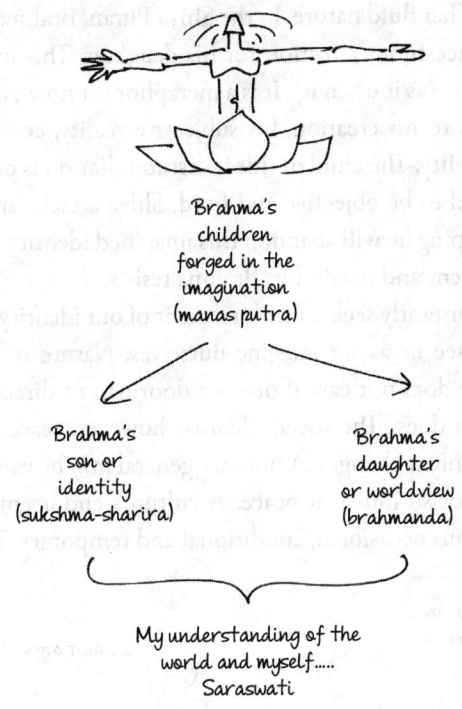

Imagination is fluid, or saras. Our imagination of the world, hence ourselves, keeps changing all the time. It will change with context or with better observation. If in one context, we may see ourselves as heroes, in another we may see ourselves as victims or martyrs. Initially, we may see the employer as a saviour; but over time, with more information, on closer inspection, we may see the employer as the oppressor and ourselves as the oppressed. From saras comes Saraswati, goddess of knowledge. Knowledge is fluid; springing from imagination, constantly shape shifting, with the potential to expand towards infinity.

In the Brahma Puran, brahmanda is referred to as Brahma's daughter, his creation. She is Shatarupa, she of many forms, a reminder of her fluid nature. In the Shiva Puran, Brahma is accused of having incestuous affection for his daughter. This must not be taken literally (as it often is). It is a metaphor for how every human being clings to his creation, his subjective reality, convinced it is objective reality. The child of this incestuous liaison is our identity, also assumed to be objective and fixed. Shiva attacks and beheads Brahma, hoping he will abandon this imagined identity that makes him dependent and needy, but Brahma resists.

We constantly seek an endorsement of our identity. We adore those who see us as we imagine ourselves. Nature refuses to do that. Nature does not care if one is a doorman or director, but an organization does. The social identity, however, ceases to matter when the context changes. A military general may be valued during a war but not so much in peace. A culture's endorsement of our identity is thus occasional, conditional and temporary. This fills us

with the fear of invalidation, a uniquely human fear, the greatest of fears that makes every human being feel dreadful, miserable and invisible.

Some react to this invalidation by seeking escape: either in work, entertainment or alcohol. Others seek an adrenaline rush to feel alive, anything from extreme sports to gambling. Still others turn to gluttony and greed, perversions and pettiness, grabbing more wealth and power in a bid to punish nature or culture itself. These may be condemned in society as vices, but they are in fact the cry of victims of imagination, desperately seeking meaning.

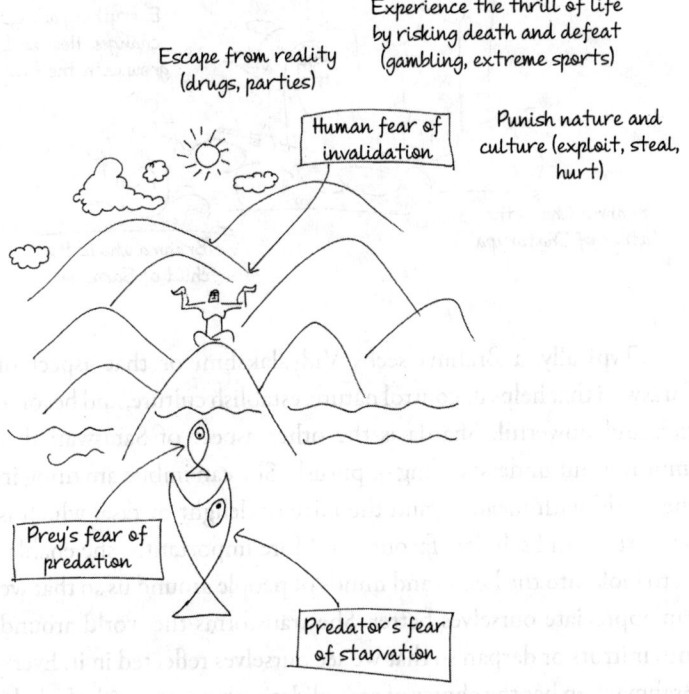

Shatarupa—imagination that amplifies our fears—can also liberate us from fear, for she is also Saraswati. In order to transform we need to stop clinging to and controlling imagination, but allow her to flow. If Brahma allows Shatarupa to be Saraswati, the trap will turn into a teacher. Saraswati will enable Brahma to outgrow fear and become the self-reliant swayambhu, like the independent Shiva and the dependable Vishnu. This can happen only if the 'father' wills it so, that is, Brahma allows himself to become the 'child'.

Typically, a Brahma seeks Vidyalakshmi or that aspect of Saraswati that helps us control nature, establish culture, and become rich and powerful. Sharda is the other aspect of Saraswati that improves our understanding of purush. She can imbue anything in the world with meaning and the juice of delight or rasa, which is why artists and scholars favour her. More importantly, she enables us to look into the hearts and minds of people around us so that we can appreciate ourselves better. She transforms the world around into mirrors or darpan so that we see ourselves reflected in it. Every Brahma then has the choice of consolidating his varna with the help of Vidyalakshmi, or outgrowing fear with Sharda, so that our guna changes from tamas through rajas towards sattva.

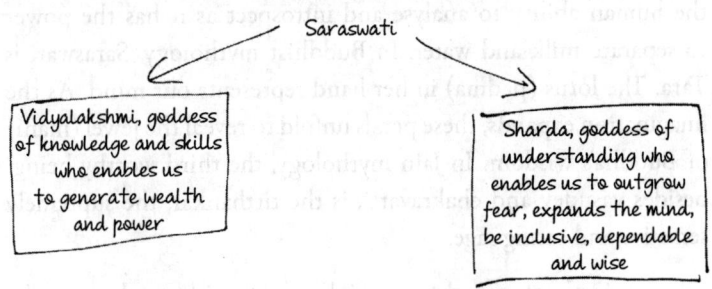

For this to happen, smriti must become shruti through tapasya. Smriti means the external voice through which information can be exchanged during the yagna. Shruti means the inner voice of our thoughts that cannot be exchanged. We communicate through smriti but we listen only to shruti. Smriti may inspire us but only shruti can transform us. Tapasya or introspection and contemplation play a key role in transforming smriti into shruti. When smriti becomes shruti, what I have becomes what I am. We no longer have power; we become powerful. We no longer have knowledge; we become wise. We do not need Durga from the outside world as we invoke Shakti within. We discover our potential within and hence find resources everywhere. We move from dependence towards dependability.

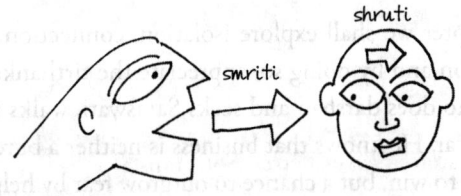

Smriti is represented by the book in Saraswati's hand while shruti by the one-stringed lute, the ik-tara that she plucks as she waits for realization to strike. Saraswati's goose or hamsa represents

The Talent Sutra

the human ability to analyse and introspect as it has the power to separate milk and water. In Buddhist mythology, Saraswati is Tara. The lotus (padma) in her hand represents our mind. As the imagination expands, these petals unfold to reveal the jewel (mani) of Buddha's wisdom. In Jain mythology, the third worthy being, besides vasudev and chakravarti, is the tirthankar, the supremely sensitive and caring sage.

- Tirthankar is the non-violent one, with no desire to be aggressive, dominating or territorial, for he can see how imagination can amplify fear and isolate humans from the rest of the world.
- He draws attention to the tirtha or ford, existing in the river of imagination, waiting to be discovered, that allows us to connect with worlds that seem otherwise separated and reflect on them.
- It is tough for a yajaman to walk across the tirtha and see the world from the devata's point of view. This demands expansion of the mind.
- It is tougher still to get the devata to walk across to the yajaman's side. Instruction is of no use. Inclusion demands we make room for even those who refuse to make room for us.

In this chapter we shall explore isolation, connection, expansion and inclusion and by doing so, appreciate the tirthankar's gaze. A yajaman who does darshan and seeks Saraswati, walks the path of the tirthankar. He knows that business is neither a burden to bear nor a battle to win, but a chance to outgrow fear by helping others outgrow theirs. This opportunity is available only to humans. To realize it is humanity's dharma.

All her life, Bela believed in an open-door policy for managers, but people rarely entered her cabin. She concluded that they were fools never to take advantage of her charitable nature. She saw herself as a misunderstood hero, until someone pointed out that everyone was intimidated by her. She was such a hard taskmaster and so demanding that people feared entering her cabin for it would invariably lead to her pulling them up for something or the other. She was the villain according to all the people who ever worked with her. Bela now had a choice: shrug her shoulders and accept the situation, as she wasn't about to change, or take responsibility for the world of fear she had unintentionally created around her. Bela chose to take responsibility and began watching how she engaged with people. She started looking at her team as a set of people, not task-completers or target-achievers. She started seeing the world from their point of view. Saraswati began to flow in Bela's head, widening her gaze, making her pay attention to the imagined realities around her and how they clashed with her own imagined reality. The more she walked the path of the tirthankar, the more she felt in charge; more of a swayambhu and less of a helpless offspring of circumstances. As Brahma, she replaced the old world of fear with a new world of encouragement much to the delight of her team.

Isolation

We want to be seen by others, but more often than not are unable to see others ourselves. We focus on making ourselves attractive. Focused on self-preservation, self-propagation and self-actualization, everyone gets isolated and wonder why they feel so lonely.

The gaze can be cruel or caring

In the Mahabharat, Duryodhan denies the Pandavs their throne while Krishna helps them reclaim it. Duryodhan abuses Draupadi, the wife of the Pandavs and Krishna rescues her. It is easy to see Duryodhan as the villain and Krishna as the hero if we restrict our gaze to these actions. If we seek the seed of the fruit, on the other hand, we can look beyond. We can wonder: what makes one man a villain and another man a hero? The epics provide some answers.

Duryodhan's father is denied the throne because he is born blind. Duryodhan's mother Gandhari blindfolds herself, as she wants to share her husband's suffering. She refuses to remove the blindfold even to look at her son because she refuses to break the vow taken during marriage. Thus Duryodhan ends up with one parent who cannot see him and the other parent who will not see

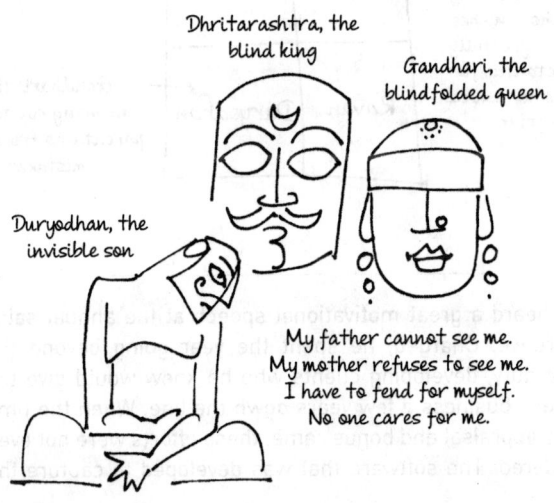

him. Unseen, Duryodhan feels uncared for. He has to fend for himself, as an animal fends for itself in the forest. Naturally, he displays animal traits: aggression, territoriality and domination. He sees the Pandavs as predators.

Krishna, on the other hand, has a childhood full of love and affection. When he broke pots, stole butter and played pranks, his mother, Yashoda, punished him but simultaneously she wept, indicating how much it pained her to punish him. In punishment, she never let him lose sight of her affection for him. That she was disciplining him did not mean he was wrong; it simply meant he had not expanded his mind to accommodate others' points of view. A child is allowed to not consider the feelings of others but an adult does not have that luxury. Krishna never felt isolated and alone. He did not see the world of humans as being full of predators and prey, as Duryodhan did.

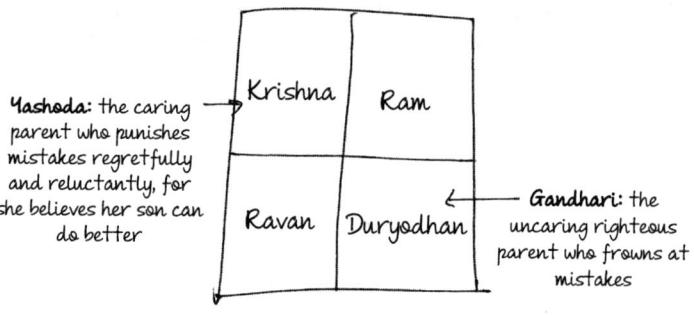

Tariq heard a great motivational speech at the annual sales conference. Charged, he spent the year going beyond the call of duty, developing clients who he knew would give the company business a few years down the line. When the time for the appraisal and bonus came, these efforts were not even considered. The software that was developed to capture the work done in the previous year had no columns for 'going beyond the call of duty'. It only measured results against organizational expectations and plans. Then the bell curve of organizational performance, achieved through a series of complex algorithms, graded Tariq far below his expectations, even below his manager's rating of him. Tariq's manager protested but to no avail. The technology for determining compensation was world-class, recommended by the best consultants in the world and implemented by the best software company in India. Its results could not be challenged. Tariq felt like a fool. Worse, he felt invisible. He realized that the shareholders of his company valued the technology more than his manager or even his manager's manager. The organization was his Gandhari who saw only his measurable deeds not his disappointment.

Everyone seeks a caring gaze

For humans, the forest is a place of fear as is the time of night. Yet, according to the Bhagavat Puran, the rasa-lila always takes place outside the village in the forest at night. Krishna plays the flute and the women leave the security of their homes to secretly be with him, dancing around him in a perfect circle. He is no brother, father, son or lover, bound by neither law nor custom and yet the women seek his company. Krishna multiplies himself for each of them, giving each one his complete and exclusive attention.

Later, Krishna moves to Dwarka, and ends up having 16,108 wives. When Narad visits the city, he finds Krishna in each of these houses, giving his full attention to all his wives and their children. He has multiplied himself once again.

The market is a frightening place. We are afraid of being cheated and exploited. We want someone to make us feel secure and wanted. Someone to validate us instead of judging us. We want to be indulged. The employee seeks individual attention from the employer; the buyer seeks individual attention from the seller. We seek Krishna in the forest, who does not use the collective as an excuse to forget the individual.

Everyone in Sanjog's team hates him. In brainstorming meetings only Sanjog speaks, not letting anyone get a word in. If the meeting lasts for an hour, he speaks for 55 minutes. When someone interrupts, they are promptly silenced. If someone disagrees, they are told they do not have the experience to understand. Sanjog is blind to his team. He is blind to himself. He does not realize that he is drawing power from his team, making them powerless. He is no Krishna. The team is far from experiencing rasa-lila.

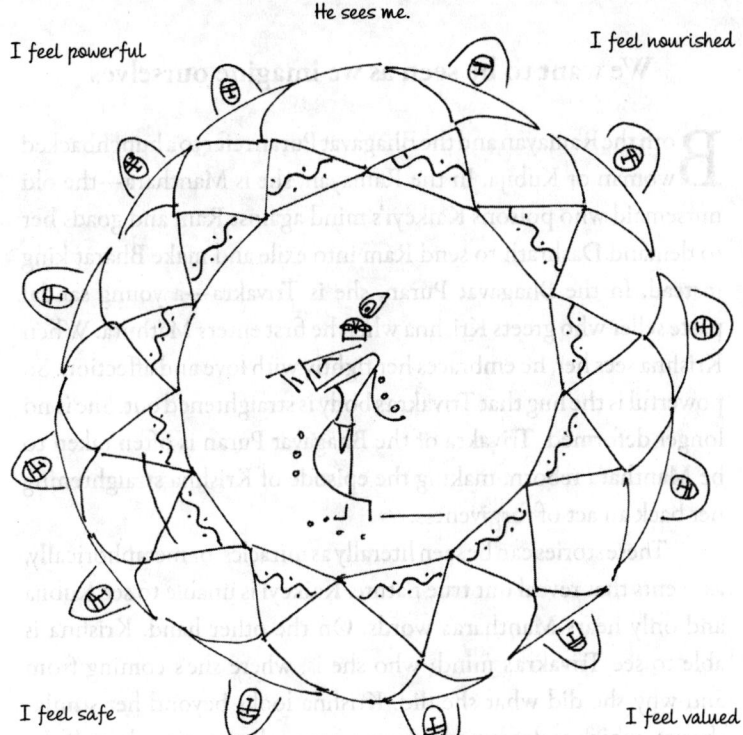

We want to be seen as we imagine ourselves

Both the Ramayan and the Bhagavat Puran refer to a hunchbacked woman or Kubija. In the Ramayan, she is Manthara—the old nursemaid who poisons Kaikeyi's mind against Ram and goads her to demand Dashrath to send Ram into exile and make Bharat king instead. In the Bhagavat Puran, she is Trivakra—a young sandal paste seller who greets Krishna when he first enters Mathura. When Krishna sees her, he embraces her tightly with love and affection. So powerful is the hug that Trivakra's body is straightened out. She is no longer deformed. Trivakra of the Bhagavat Puran is often taken to be Manthara reborn, making the episode of Krishna straightening her back an act of forgiveness.

These stories can be seen literally as miracles, or metaphorically, as events that reveal our true nature. Kaikeyi is unable to see Kubija and only hears Manthara's words. On the other hand, Krishna is able to see Trivakra's mind: who she is, where she's coming from and why she did what she did. Krishna looks beyond her sthula-sharira, which is deformed. He sees her as she imagines herself; he sees her suksma-sharira. He finds her as beautiful and innocent as she thinks she is. So he hugs her, expresses his affection for her, provides her the security she so desperately needs. She may not be like others but that does not mean she needs any less validation. Having got it from Krishna, she no longer feels like an outsider or an ugly person who can only get the master's attention and affection through manipulation.

The workplace is full of Kubijas. In a world where only performance seems to matter, they are mediocre, at the wrong end of the bell curve, people who can be justifiably kicked out. And this makes them insecure. The only way then to secure their job is to have a relationship with people in power, display loyalty by poisoning their ears against others, making the yajaman feel there is someone looking out for them.

Every year, the Clark Travel Company selects two management trainees. This year they have selected Meghna and Rose. Meghna comes from an affluent family and this job is a way for her to pass her time before she gets married. She, therefore, resents it when her manager piles work on her and makes her stay late on weekends. Rose comes from a very poor family and has been able to go to college thanks to the kindness of relatives. She is deeply in debt. She is very grateful for the job, anxious about losing it and eager to please. Her boss keeps finding fault with her work and that frightens her further. Both Meghna and Rose feel unloved like Kubija and yearn for a Krishna who will see them for who they truly are.

A cruel gaze focuses on our compliance rather than our capability

Hanuman plays a crucial role in the Ramayan. He is asked to discover Sita's whereabouts, build a bridge across the sea with the aid of the monkeys, fetch the lifesaving herbs that save Lakshman's life—all of which he accomplishes. Throughout the epic, he proves his capability time and again. He is strong enough to carry mountains and smart enough to trick sea-monsters like Surasa and Simhika.

Yet in the epic, he does not hold any great position. He is just one of the many monkeys Ram encounters in the forest. He is not Sugriva, leader of the monkey troop. He is not Angad, son of Vali, who is told to lead the band of monkeys searching for Sita. He is not Jambavan, the bear, or Nila, the monkey, who are given the responsibility of building the bridge. At no point does Hanuman make any attempt to steal anyone's glory; while in his own temple he stands powerful with a mountain in his hand and his feet on a demon, in Ram's temple he is most content sitting at the feet of his master, hands in supplication.

Who would not want a Hanuman on his team? The perfect karya-karta, one who is very good at his work, one who will do whatever he is told without ever seeking either reward or recognition; one who finds validation in obeying his master.

Years after the events in the Ramayan took place, Hanuman narrates the entire tale to his mother, Anjani. After hearing everything that's transpired, she wonders aloud, "Why did they go through the trouble of raising an army and building a bridge to defeat Ravan? Why did you not simply flick your tail and sweep the rakshasa-king and his army away?"

Hanuman replies, "Because no one asked me to."

And suddenly we wonder if this was a lost opportunity. Everyone saw Hanuman's obedience, but no one saw his true potential. Everyone saw Hanuman on their terms, not on his terms. In a world that celebrates alignment and compliance to the vision, systems and processes of an organization, is the individual increasingly getting invisible?

Unless the yajaman pays attention to the potential of the devata, the yagna achieves only a portion of what it could potentially achieve. The tathastu stays limited by the yajaman's gaze.

At Raju's auto-repair shop, all the work is done by his Hanuman: Amol, a young boy, who has been working with Raju for three years. Amol is a natural, able to fix the most complex of problems. Raju knows he can totally rely on Amol. No job is too big or too small for Amol. He is as happy changing a tyre as he is fixing the brakes. He does not boss over the juniors and does not feel slighted if the seniors ask him to fetch tea. If there is a problem that eludes a standard solution, everyone knows to leave it to Amol. He will, like Hanuman crossing the sea, find a way. Yes, Raju loves Amol's work. Yes, Raju admires Amol's work. But is Raju harnessing Amol's full potential?

The Talent Sutra

Unseen, we are compelled to fend for ourselves

A fisherman catches a river fish, inside which he finds, miraculously, a pair of twins: a boy and a girl. The fisherman takes the children to Ushinara, the childless king of the land. The king adopts the boy, not the girl. She is named Satyavati and raised among the fishermen.

When Satyavati grows up she ferries people across the river. Shantanu, the old king of Hastinapur, falls in love with her and wants to marry her, but the leader of the fishermen says, "Only if her sons inherit your throne."

Shantanu has a son called Devavrat from an earlier marriage. To make his father happy, Devavrat gives up his claim to the throne, paving the way for Satyavati to marry his father. "But what if your children fight my children?" says Satyavati.

The roots of Satyavati's ambitions lay in her rejection by Ushinara who preferred the male child to the female child. She, who was not allowed to be princess, now wants to be queen and

mother of kings. She wants to be seen as she imagines herself.

Our desire to achieve does not happen in isolation. We seek an audience. When the audience refuses to cheer for us, we work hard until they admire us. We validate ourselves, like Satyavati, through the Other. The Other is the parent whose attention we crave.

Nandita's dream has come true. She is a successful television actress. She has the best role she could have ever imagined and she is paid very well. The days of struggle are over. The audiences love her, as indicated by the ratings of her show. Still, every day she throws tantrums on the sets. She arrives late, refuses to come out of her trailer until the director begs her to, demands audiences with the television channel head, and insists on changing dialogues at the last minute. Unless she does this, she feels she is not being given her due. She is worth so much more. She was happiest when a trade journal revealed that she was the highest paid television star in history. She felt she had finally been seen.

The Talent Sutra

We refuse to see ourselves as villains

Naraka, the asura, attacks Amravati and drives Indra out, laying claim to the treasures of paradise. Indra seeks the help of Vishnu and gets anxious when there is no sign of him in Vaikuntha. He is directed to Krishna, who lives on earth, and is considered to be Vishnu incarnate.

Indra doubts Krishna's divinity but, desperate, seeks his help anyway. To his surprise, Krishna summons and mounts the eagle Garud and, with his wife Satyabhama by his side, rises to the sky bearing his resplendent weapons to battle with Naraka. After an intense battle, Krishna manages to vanquish Naraka and Indra regains his kingdom.

Naraka is no ordinary asura. He is the son of the earth-goddess, Bhudevi, and Varaha, the boar avatar of Vishnu who had rescued Bhudevi from the bottom of the sea after she had been dragged there by the asura, Hiranayaksha. When Krishna kills Naraka, Vishnu effectively kills his own son, but Indra is not even aware of this.

While leaving, Satyabhama expresses her desire for the parijata tree that grows in Indra's courtyard. Indra, however, refuses to part with it. Indra's refusal shocks Satyabhama who now becomes adamant about taking the tree back with her to earth. So Krishna takes it by force. When Indra tries to stop Krishna, another battle follows, this time with the devas, in which Indra is predictably defeated.

The story reveals the character of Indra. He is desperate to get help from Krishna but is unwilling to share even a tree with his saviour. He wants things, but never gives things. The king of the devas is not known for his generosity. He clings to his paradise but cannot enjoy it as he continuously fears losing it. His clinginess creates circumstances that contribute to his losing control over Amravati. When he manages to get it back with a little help from Vishnu, he returns to his clingy ways. Misfortune makes him miserable but fortune does not make him gracious. Circumstances teach him nothing as he is convinced he has nothing to learn. When this is pointed out, people like Indra simply shrug their shoulders, become defensive and say: we are like this only.

And so at the workplace, Indra comes to your workstation only because he wants something. He expects you to do it because that is your job. But when you ask him for something, he refuses to help as he feels you are asking for a favour.

When Murli calls John, John knows that there is trouble in the family. Murli is one of the star directors of a family business and John is the head of accounts. Whenever the family members have a fight Murli calls John and spends hours saying nasty things about the family, claiming they are ganging up against him. John knows never to take these things seriously. Once the family dispute is settled, Murli will stop calling John and start maligning John lest John reveal what was said in those earlier phone calls. Everybody thinks that John is close to the family but John knows that no matter how loyal he is, how well he performs, he will never ever be a member of the family, never a shareholder of the company, regardless of the many promises made by Murli. John's wife says he should ask for his rights. "Rights?" John replies with amusement, "I only have a salary that I get paid every month. Everything else is just wishful thinking." John knows that Indra will not part with his parijata tree. John also knows he is no Krishna capable of overpowering his Indra.

We use work as a beacon to get attention

After Valmiki writes the Ramayan, he learns that Hanuman has also written a Ramayan. Curious about Hanuman's version, he goes to the distant plantain forest in the warm valleys cradled by the Himalayas where Hanuman lives.

There he finds the banana leaf on which Hanuman has etched his version of Ram's tale. The vocabulary, grammar, melody and metre are so perfect that Valmiki starts to cry, "After reading Hanuman's Ramayan, nobody will read Valmiki's Ramayan." On hearing this, Hanuman tears the banana leaf with the epic on it, crushes it into a ball, pops it into his mouth and swallows it. "Why did you do that?" asks a surprised Valmiki.

Hanuman replies, "You need your Ramayan more than I need my Ramayan. You wrote your Ramayan because you want the world to remember you. I wrote my Ramayan because I wanted to remember Ram."

Ram embodies Narayan, human potential. Valmiki is nara, the human being. Hanuman is vanar, a monkey and an animal—less than human because he is not blessed with the power of imagination. Still, it is Hanuman who sees his work as an exercise to discover what he is capable of becoming while Valmiki sees his work as a beacon to gather fame, attention and validation. Hanuman seeks Narayan while Valmiki seeks Narayani. Narayan helps us see others. Narayani gets others to see us.

It is important to remind ourselves of who it is we work for. While the official purpose of work is to satisfy customers, employers, employees, shareholders and family, the unofficial purpose of work is to satisfy ourselves, feel noticed and alive.

Our work can become the tool that helps us grow not just materially but also emotionally and intellectually. It can widen our gaze. Valmiki, without realizing it, focuses only on material growth; Hanuman focuses on emotional and intellectual growth. When we widen our gaze, material growth follows. But the reverse is not true.

My writing reveals my communication skills (Vidyalakshmi)

As I write about Ram, I realize how much potential I still have to realize (Sharda)

Lakotiaji has established some of the finest educational institutions in areas that did not have, until twenty years ago, even a decent primary school. Because of him many children have been educated and many adults have got jobs. The business has made him very rich, a much-respected member of the community. But Lakotiaji is upset. "The government has not recognized me. I deserve a Padma Shri." He is currently lobbying local politicians and the media hoping someone will recommend his name.

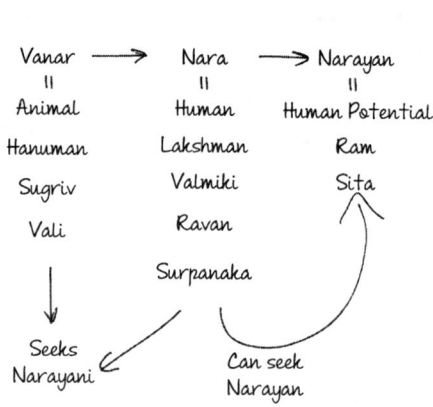

Our goals justify our lack of a caring gaze

In the Mahabharat, every character is invisible. Nobody sees anybody. Everyone is too busy gazing at ideals and institutions until Krishna arrives.

Bhisma sacrifices property and conjugal rights so that his old father, Shantanu, can marry Satyavati. Before long, the celibate and childless Bhisma finds himself responsible for Satyavati's children, grandchildren and great-grandchildren. Since he sacrificed everything to please his father, he expects the children of the household to display similar selflessness and nobility. Fears and insecurities of individual family members are dismissed as being self-indulgent. So fixed is his gaze on the family name that the family members feel small and invalidated.

Before long, the gaze of his great-grandchildren shrinks. The Pandavs and Kauravs start seeing the kingdom as their property more than responsibility. They start valuing the kingdom more than each other. This marks the downfall of the household. But at no point does anyone see the venerable ancestor's sacrifice as contributing to the downward spiral. Even Bhisma blames external influences for family problems, never once gazing upon his own gaze.

Often leaders are so consumed by their personal values and agendas that they expect their followers to be as excited about what matters to them. They get angry with followers who resist or refuse to keep pace. Those who align with their goals are celebrated. The rest are condemned as selfish.

For many, the whole purpose of existence is self-actualization and thus they voluntarily isolate themselves from the rest of the ecosystem. Nothing matters except their goals and ambitions. Achieving them makes them heroes while the failure to do so makes them martyrs. No one looks at the string of disappointed faces and broken hearts that they leave behind in their wake. Feelings don't matter when we do business, we are told. We are taught to believe that if it is not personal, it is okay to hurt.

At the open house session, the staff of an organization that sold mobile toilets complained that they were being forced to work overtime. They were promised a half-day on Saturday, but they ended up working late. The owner, Purab, shouted, "I work much more than you do, twice as much, so I expect you to give more. Isn't this work noble? We are liberating people from the humiliation of open toilets. How can you ask for holidays when there are people who do not have even basic amenities?" The staff immediately kept quiet. No one pointed out that they were not shareholders, they were not going to get a share of the profit and that their salaries would not rise proportionately if the business grew. They did not care for Purab's ideals or vision. They felt embarrassed telling their families about their jobs. The staff felt that Purab would see such candid views as subversive and threatening so they kept quiet, submitting to what each one imagined to be exploitation. Purab kept grumbling about the absence of ownership amongst the staff for the noble vision of his organization. Purab is Bhisma, so blinded by his vision that he does not see his staff is made of Indras seeking higher returns with low investment. He refuses to see how, for centuries, Indians have always looked down upon those who clean toilets.

I am but a resource

Reflection

When we genuinely see others, we realize that they are often responding to their perceptions of us. How they see us is very different from how we see ourselves. As we contemplate this, we understand the world and appreciate ourselves better.

Fear isolates us while imagination connects us

The Garud Puran refers to a river called Vaitarni, which separates the living from the dead. This is the metaphorical river of fear that surrounds every brahmanda separating it from the other brahmandas.

The word 'tirtha' refers to a ford, a shallow part of the river that allows one to cross over to the other side. Unlike a bridge that needs to be built, a ford exists naturally and has to be discovered. Imagination is the ford that enables a yajaman to explore the devata's brahmanda and even reflect on how his own brahmanda appears from the other side. Tirtha transforms Vaitarni, the river of fear that separates, into Saraswati, the river of knowledge that connects. The yajaman who discovers the tirtha and walks on it is the tirthankar. In Jain scriptures, all worthy beings are classified as:

- Those who are action-driven like the vasudev who fights the prati-vasudev since his pacifist brother, the baladev, refuses to.

- Those who are rule-driven or the chakravartis.
- Those who are thought-driven or the tirthankars.

The tirthankar can see that while the vasudev feels like a hero and views the prati-vasudev as villain, the prati-vasudev sees himself as a leader, the chakravarti or keeper of the universal order. For the chakravarti, the vasudev is no hero; he is a rule-breaker, a threat to order. Neither sees the other. Vaitarni isolates each one. Unless they walk over the tirtha, there will always be conflict and violence in their relationship.

For the tirthankar, the other serves as a mirror or darpan. In them, he sees reflected aspects of his own personality and his own fears. If he judges these feelings, and choices, he will deny them, indulge them, justify them, fight them, but never outgrow them. To outgrow them, he has to accept their existence and be at peace. This is non-violence.

We often see the world through our own prejudices. The realization that everyone does the same thing should prompt us to observe other people's prejudices and wonder why they feel the way they do, rather than simply dismissing them. The chakravarti is too busy finding fault in vasudev, and the vasudev too busy fighting the prati-vasudev. Should the chakravarti invest more time in wondering why vasudev looks upon him as prati-vasudev, and should the vasudev invest more time in wondering why not everyone looks at the king as the villain, both would walk the path of the tirthankar.

Urvashi started a toy business. She could see huge potential both locally and internationally, but she could not scale up her business as government policies saw it as a cottage industry. These laws were instituted to protect and encourage small players. But these laws were shortsighted and they did not stop international players from supporting their toy industry and enabling them to create products at low rates and exporting them to other markets. As cheap foreign toys flooded the market, Urvashi lost her competitive edge in the market. Urvashi begged the government to intervene and the banks to reconsider their policies. But like stern chakravartis the bureaucrats and ministers refused to budge. Urvashi sees the government as prati-vasudev, the obstacle to her chance of being a successful entrepreneur. She had to close down her business and take up a job once again.

We often forget that others see the world differently

After the war at Kurukshetra, where the Pandavs defeat the Kauravs, there is an argument as to who is responsible for the victory. Is it Arjun who killed the mighty Kaurav commanders Bhisma, Jayadhrata and Karna? Or is it Bhim who killed the hundred Kaurav brothers? No one can decide, so they turn to the talking head on top of the hill overlooking the battlefield.

This is the head of a warrior who was decapitated before he entered the battlefield. He so longed to see the war that, taking pity on him, Krishna had his head put atop a hill. From this vantage point, he could see everything that happened in the battle over eighteen days.

When asked who was the greater warrior, the talking head said, "I did not see Bhim or Arjun. I did not see the Pandavs or Kauravs. I only saw Vishnu's discus severing the necks of corrupt kings and the earth-goddess stretching out her tongue to drink their blood."

In our yearning to be seen, we assume our own importance, until someone comes along and reminds us that we are but part of the big picture. Our roles in our departments sometimes become so important that we forget that we are part of a bigger picture. Our transaction that causes us great joy or pain is merely one of the thousands of transactions that are part of our enterprise.

People who have been in line-functions or customer-facing functions resist doing desk jobs in special projects or corporate offices. This is usually a good thing in one's career, at least for a short duration. But by working for some time in the HR department or finance department or CEO's office, they get a wider view of the organization and are able to contextualize the roles of those on the frontline. Somehow, from the dizzy heights of Kailas, the frenzy in Kashi seems insignificant.

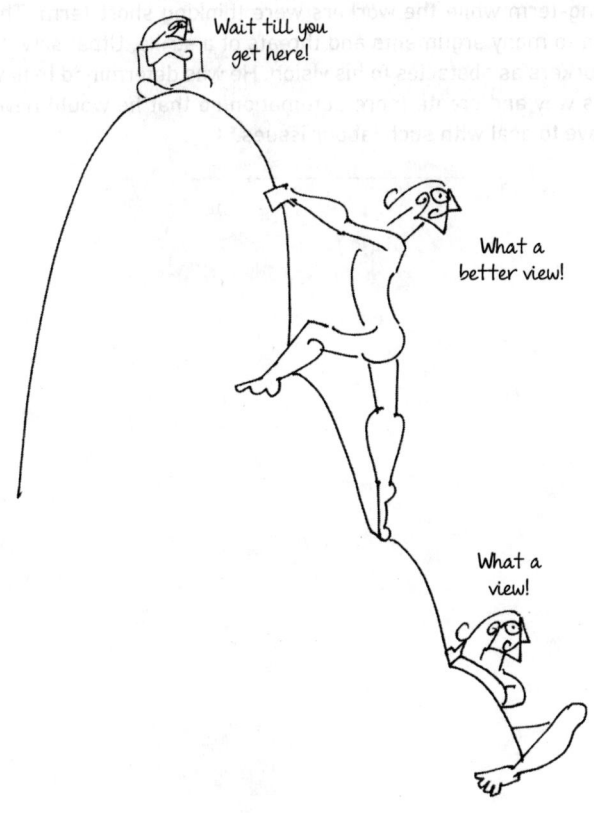

When Utpal's company made 40 per cent profits, the workers expected a 40 per cent bonus. But they received only a 10 per cent bonus, barely enough to account for inflation. The workers protested. Utpal explained he needed the profits to build another factory that would allow him to increase capacity and lower the cost of goods produced, which would enable him to stay competitive in the markets. But the workers felt this was an elaborate argument to deny them their dues. And how would they benefit from a larger factory? Utpal was thinking long-term while the workers were thinking short-term. This led to many arguments and threats of a strike. Utpal saw the workers as obstacles to his vision. He was determined to have his way and create more automation so that he would never have to deal with such labour issues.

How we see others reveals who we are

In the forest, while searching for Sita who had been abducted by Ravan, Ram and Lakshman meet an old lady called Shabari who invites them to a meal in her house. She offers them her frugal meal: berries she has collected in the forest.

Lakshman is horrified to see Shabari taking a bite of each berry before passing it on to his brother. Sometimes, she does not even pass the berry and just throws it away. "How dare you give leftover food to my brother?" Lakshman snarls. "Do you know who he is? He is Ram of the Raghu clan, King of Ayodhya!" An embarrassed Shabari throws herself at Ram's feet and apologizes for her mistake.

Ram looks at Lakshman with amazement, "What are you seeing, Lakshman? Here is a woman who is sharing the best of the food she has gathered for herself with two complete strangers, armed men at that. And you are angry with her? Look at her: she lives in the forest, and you expect her to know palace etiquette. She is biting the berries to make sure she feeds us the sweetest, most succulent ones. And instead of appreciating her generosity and kindness, you are angry with her! What does that say about you? Ayodhya and the Raghu clan may be important to you but they mean nothing to her. You expect her to see me as you see me. But do you really see me? Do you see anything except the way you imagine the world?"

The way Lakshman sees Shabari says nothing about Shabari; it reveals everything about Lakshman. The decisions, instructions and attitude of a yajaman reveal how he sees the yagna and the devata, and his own role. More often than not, a workplace is full of Lakshmans, ready to judge and instruct the Other, unlike Ram who appreciates people for who they are.

Many leaders insist that their assistant leave a small note about the background of the person they are about to meet before the meeting takes place. This ensures they do not make any blunders during the conversation and they are able to give the person they are meeting the impression that they matter, that they have been seen.

At a team meeting, the junior-most trainee proposed an idea. "That is ridiculous," snapped the chief operating officer, Qureishi. Later, during a coffee break, the chief executive officer, Ansari, took Qureishi aside and said, "By ridiculing that trainee's proposal you have frightened everyone in the team. Now they will not be free with their ideas. They will be wary of what you may say. No one wants to look foolish. Imagine the trainee was brave enough to open up in front of the top management. Instead of appreciating him, you have mocked him. Made him feel even smaller than the junior status he currently occupies in the organization. You saw his proposal objectively, I understand. I wish you had seen it subjectively. Then you would not have demotivated him." Like Lakshman, Qureishi had failed to see the courage of the trainee. Now he realized why Ansari was such a favourite with everyone in the organization. It was not just the position he held. Ansari never ridiculed anyone; he never made anyone feel small. He genuinely valued everyone's ideas and helped each one see why it could, or could not be, implemented.

How others see us reveals who we are

Surya, the sun-god, was horrified when he noticed that the woman in his house was not his wife, Saranya, but her shadow, Chhaya. He stormed to the house of his father-in-law for an explanation, only to learn that she had run away because she could not bear his celestial radiance.

Surya realized that while in his story he was the victim, according to his wife he was the villain. That she had slipped away in secret and left a duplicate behind in her place was an indicator of the extent of her fear. Had he seen the world from her point of view, he would have realized beforehand what had frightened his wife before she had taken the drastic step of running away.

Surya then sought out his wife, and discovered she had taken the form of a mare. Instead of asking her to change back to human form, he turned into a horse and followed her to the pasture.

Yes, he could expect his wife to accept him as he was, or compel her to change for him, but that would mean he was incapable of growth. Reflecting on the other person's viewpoint prompts Surya to discover his ability to adapt, accommodate and grow. From god, he becomes animal and leads a happy life in the pasture until Saranya is able to once more return to the sky by his side as his goddess.

This story reveals how the behaviour of people around us is a reaction to how they perceive us. If they fear us, they behave in a certain way. If they trust us, they behave differently. All behaviour depends on how other people perceive us. We can demand of others that they change their perceptions of us or we can decide to change ourselves and work on being more trustworthy. In the latter choice lies growth.

People often wonder why they are treated with respect in

office and not the same way at home. It is usually an indicator of the power structures in the family and workplace. If we are feared in the family, everyone obeys us. If we are feared in the office, everyone tiptoes around us. If we are cruel to family members, it usually indicates that we feel they do not see us as we would wish to be seen or listen to us. The Other is always the mirror, the darpan, in which we can have a darshan of ourselves.

	I am...	He is...	
1.	Tiger	Tiger	Conflict
2.	Tiger	Goat	I dominate him
3.	Goat	Tiger	He dominates me
4.	Goat	Goat	We graze together
5.	Human	Whatever	I can include him even if he does not include me

---

For two years, Sandesh had headed the operations department and put in place a whole set of systems and processes. With great difficulty, he had managed to get his team to align with the new environment and the results had been spectacular. Then Sandesh decided to spend more time on strategic thinking and appointed Ketan to handle the operations role. He just had to ensure the systems and processes set up over two years were being followed. But no sooner had Sandesh handed over the reins of the company than everything went awry. No one followed processes or systems and all reports came in late. Sandesh was angry with Ketan and his team for failing to do their jobs. Then he realized the event revealed something about him. He had instituted the new processes by force of his personality. Alignment happened because people followed him, not the process. So, when Ketan replaced him, everything collapsed. Ketan did not have the same force of personality as he did. No matter how much he blamed Ketan and his team, he was the source of the problem. Now, he had to go back to focusing on operations. But this time, like Surya, he had to change himself. Coach people to do the tasks not because he told them to, but because it was work that had to be done; in other words, take ownership. He also had to work with Ketan so that Ketan could take on the huge responsibility without feeling abandoned. By this singular shift in thinking, Sandesh had created a growth opportunity for himself.

The Other reveals the power of our gaze

Rishabh is a highly revered king who is invited by Indra to Amravati to attend a dance recital. It turns out to be an outstanding performance. Rishabh is enthralled by the skill of the dancer, but suddenly, in the middle of the performance, the dancer dies. Indra uses his magic power to make the dead dancer disappear and replaces her with another. It happens so fast that no one notices except Rishabh. It makes him wonder.

Why does Indra do what he does? Where does the need to hide the truth come from? Rishabh realizes that for all his outward pomp and glory, Indra imagines himself as prey. He needs to secure himself with this magic trick. Who does Indra imagine as his predator? Rishabh realizes that in Indra's eyes he is the tiger. This takes Rishabh by surprise, as he thinks of himself as a benevolent king. Is Rishabh's imagination of himself truer than Indra's imagination of him?

Indra's image of Rishabh is born out of fear. Maybe, Rishabh, without realizing it, is contributing to Indra's fear. Rishabh comes across as self-righteous and noble, with clearly a higher level of ethics and morality than Indra, and this makes Indra insecure. Rishabh sees how imagination creates the jungle even when there is none. In the mind's eye, predators appear to be seeking prey, and alphas appear to be seeking domination.

This event transforms Rishabh into a tirthankar, for he sees clearly the violence of thoughts. He decides to renounce this violence and outgrow every underlying fear. He decides to spend his time observing the realm of thoughts so that he can understand and accommodate everyone he meets rather than trying to combat them. It is important to note that the event has no impact on Indra who stays the same.

Our presence impacts those around us. We may see them in one way. They see us in another. We may think we are helping while they think we are being patronizing. In each one's brahmanda, the Brahma is always right.

Ipsita notices that the way her secretary, Siddharth, speaks to her is very different from the way he speaks to the peons in office. In front of her, Siddharth is deferential and gentle whereas with the peons he is rude and imperious. Ipsita realizes that he sees her as alpha and respects her power. But he wants to position himself as alpha in front of the peons thus establishing a pecking order in the office. Ipsita has no desire to dominate Siddharth; she wants a transparent and professional relationship. But she cannot control Siddharth's worldview. Siddharth can turn the most professional workplace into a feudal order in no time. Upon introspection, Ipsita realizes that she does enjoy his deference to a degree. And by enjoying it she is contributing to the power equation. Now she realizes how expats who praise the equality in workplaces abroad, enjoy the servility of their team when they are posted to India. Unlike Rishabh, Ipsita enjoys being feared. It makes her feel powerful.

The Other reveals our insensitivity

In the Mahabharat, news reached King Virata of Matsya that his son, Uttar, had singlehandedly defeated the Kaurav army, pushing back great warriors like Karna and Duryodhan. The city prepared to welcome the young prince—the streets were watered, the buildings decorated with flowers, lamps and fluttering flags. King Virata's heart was filled with pride. His son had done the impossible. He ordered the poets to compose songs in Uttar's honour.

"But sir," said a priest standing next to Virata, "Does it not seem odd that a slip of a boy was able to defeat such mighty warriors? Surely he had help. Maybe that of his charioteer, Brihanalla, the eunuch, who once served Arjun, the great archer." The king ignored what the priest had to say and continued praising his son. Once again the priest said, "Surely sir, you do not believe he did it all alone. He must have had the support of another, perhaps Brihanalla, the eunuch, who once served Arjun, the great archer." Again the king ignored him and continued praising his son. When the priest suggested that the prince may have been helped by the eunuch-charioteer one more time, the king reacted violently. "Shut up!" he shouted, and slapped the priest so hard that his nose started to bleed.

The priest had been speaking the truth. Uttar was indeed helped by the eunuch-charioteer, Brihanalla, who was actually Arjun in disguise. But the king was not ready to hear the truth. He wanted to enjoy the alleged success of his son but the priest, in his relentless pursuit of correctness, did not appreciate a father's desire. The priest's truth was cold and insensitive. The king wanted compassion, at the cost of the truth, for some time at least.

The priest was Yudhishtir in disguise. This event takes place in the final year of exile of the Pandavs when they have to lose their identity and live incognito. The humiliation revealed to Yudhishtir the human desire for delusions and the importance of being gentle with the harsh truth. Yudhishtir was so caught up with his honesty that he did not realize the other's inability to receive it.

The ability to communicate with a king with deference and dexterity is known in Sanskrit as sabha-chaturya, which translated literally means 'tactfulness in court'. It is a trait that ministers and courtiers had to possess if they wished to survive in court and get their jobs done. It is a trait that people who work with leaders must possess. It is a trait that even leaders need to possess if they wish to lead.

The foundation for this skill lies in the observation that people are uncomfortable with the truth, especially when it shows them in a bad light or has consequences that could affect them adversely. When confronted with it, they react negatively—with rage or denial. They may get defensive or simply reject the submission. So the work does not get done. One needs strategic communication, also known as diplomacy. One needs sabha-chaturya.

Rathodji mastered the art of sabha-chaturya long ago. He knew his boss, Mr Khilachand, was a brilliant man with a rags-to-riches story. He also knew his boss had an ego the size of a mountain. He refused to accept or admit a mistake. In fact, if a mistake was pointed out, he would do everything in his power to justify it. Mr Khilachand was very fond of a distant cousin of his. So when a candidate presented himself before Mr Khilachand with a recommendation from this cousin, he was, without much consideration, appointed manager in one of the many oil depots he owned. The candidate was a good-for-nothing layabout. He did no work and impeded the smooth running of operations. But no one dared complain to Mr Khilachand. To do so would imply that Mr Khilachand was a fool for having appointed a candidate purely on a recommendation, without checking credentials. And Mr Khilachand did not appreciate being taken for a fool. In a rage, just to prove he was right—and everyone else who thought he was a fool was wrong—he could simply sack the person who had complained and give the incompetent candidate he had hired a raise or promotion. It was irrational, but that's the way he was. Rathodji knew this and so when the problem was presented to him, he pondered long and hard on how to give Mr Khilachand the message without upsetting him and making matters worse.

The Other reveals our inadequacy

As Ravan lies mortally wounded on the battlefield and the monkeys are celebrating their victory, Ram turns to his brother, Lakshman, and tells him to learn whatever he can from the rakshasa-king who is a renowned scholar. Lakshman obeys but returns soon after saying the arrogant Ravan turned his face away when asked to share his knowledge.

Ram looks at his brother and asks him, "Where did you stand while asking him for knowledge?" Lakshman replies, "Next to his head so that I could hear what he had to say clearly." Ram smiles, places his bow on the ground and walks over to where Ravan lies and, to Lakshman's astonishment, kneels at Ravan's feet.

With palms joined in extreme humility, Ram says, "Lord of Lanka, you abducted my wife, a terrible crime for which I have been forced to punish you. Now, you are no more my enemy. I bow to you and request you to share your knowledge with me."

To Lakshman's greater astonishment, Ravan opens his eyes and raises his arms to salute Ram. "If only I had more time as your teacher than as your enemy. Standing at my feet as a student, unlike your rude younger brother, you are a worthy recipient of my knowledge." Ravan then shared his vast knowledge and died.

Despite having fought against Ravan for as long as Ram did, Lakshman never saw Ravan for who he was. He did not see Ravan's desire to dominate everyone around him. He did not see what made Ravan cling to Sita even when the army of monkeys killed his brothers, his sons, his subjects, and threatened his city. Would such a man share his knowledge freely? Ram can see Ravan's need to dominate even as he is dying. That is what stops Ravan from being unconditionally generous with his knowledge. So Ram indulges the rakshasa-king, grants him the power he so desperately needs in svaha and receives Ravan's knowledge as tathastu.

Yes, in an ideal world, we should not encourage delusions. Everything should be factual. Ravan should be told that he is being mean and petty on his deathbed. But this is not an ideal world and delusions enable us to cope with the harshness of reality. Fear makes us crave delusions. Delusions grant value. Without delusions there would be no want, no market for luxury goods, no need for brands, no room for advertising.

> The attendant at the ticket counter was being very rude, but Manish said nothing. He kept smiling even though he wanted to shout back. He realized that the attendant had no other place to get Durga from and so was trying to be overly imperious. If he behaved deferentially, he would get his ticket changed quickly and not be subjected to a bout of unnecessary harassment. No, this was not right. He could complain to the station manager. But that would be a waste of time. He was not here to change the world. He just wanted to get his work done and move on. So he gave the attendant a good dose of Durga and got his Lakshmi in exchange. The attendant felt like Indra in Amravati: his job gave him more than his salary; it gave him the respect that he did not get at home or from his superiors.

The Other reveals our blindness

Karna's mother, Kunti, a princess, abandons him at birth. He is raised in a charioteer's family but he learns archery and becomes a warrior of great repute by his own merit. All the kings and warriors of the land taunt him about his lowly origins. But Duryodhan, the eldest Kaurav, makes him commander of his armies on the battlefield of Kurukshetra and even compels Shalya, king of Madra, to serve as charioteer. "You who have been called a charioteer's son all your life, shall ride into battle, bow in hand, with a king serving as your charioteer," says Duryodhan to Karna.

Blinded by his victimhood, overwhelmed by Kaurav generosity, Karna does not realize the folly of this decision. For Shalya is the uncle of the Pandavs, tricked by Duryodhan into serving the Kauravs. While Shalya is legally bound to serve Duryodhan, in spirit he favours his enemies. So as they ride into battle, Shalya keeps praising Arjun and demotivating Karna.

Then, when the chariot wheel gets stuck in the ground, Shalya says, "I am no charioteer. I am a king. I do not know how to pull out wheels stuck in the ground. Only charioteers like you know what to do." So Karna is forced to abandon his bow, get down from the chariot and pull the chariot wheel out. While Karna is thus unarmed and vulnerable, Krishna directs Arjun to take advantage of the situation and shoot Karna dead. As the arrow rips through his heart, Karna sees something that was always before him but he had never really seen: Krishna!

Born in a royal family, taunted for being raised by cowherds, Krishna was comfortable serving as a 'lowly' charioteer. Social status made no dent on his mental body. Karna finally realized what really matters in life is Narayan, not Narayani, what a person is, not what a person has.

Our imagination binds us and blinds us. We get trapped in brahmanda and do not see how limited our gaze is. It makes us heroic in our eyes, but villainous to others. Karna can be celebrated as a victim and a hero. Yet Krishna has him killed. Not because he is a villain but because defeat is the final way to open his eyes and expand his gaze. This is 'uddhar', upliftment of thought.

When Mark came to India, he noticed that most of his friends had servants: someone to clean the house, a cook, a driver, and someone to even take the children to school. "This is so feudal," he commented. Sridhar did not take the remark kindly. "Why is it not feudal when you outsource work you do not want to do to India? Are we not the cleaning ladies of the developed world? Why is hiring a servant bad but encouraging the service-industry good? When I employ a servant I am creating employment in my country. But when you outsource, you are creating unemployment in yours." Mark merely chuckled at this defensive retort but wondered later if there was a measure of truth to what Sridhar had said.

Expansion

Growth happens when we make the journey from being dependent to being dependable. This happens when we focus on who we are rather than what we have: how much we can accommodate the Other, even if the Other does not accommodate us.

Growth happens when the mind expands

Humans are called manavas because they possess manas, a mind that can imagine, hence expand. A non-expanding limited mind is identified as Brahma. An infinitely expanded limitless mind is identified as the brahman. As Brahma makes the journey towards the brahman, the mind acquires four colours or varna:

- Shudra-varna: the obedient gaze of unconditional followership, like a dog who adores his master and is eager to please him, wagging his tail when acknowledged and whining when ignored. Shudra-varna is also associated with the eternally anxious deer, seeking a herd. This is tamas-guna, as it indicates the absence of thought and a preference for mimicry. It is the varna of a newborn child. Everyone is born in this varna.
- Vaishya-varna: the merchant's calculating gaze of conditional followership like an elephant that follows the oldest matriarch in the herd as she has lived through the most droughts and therefore has more knowledge of waterholes than the others. This is rajas-guna, as the merchant thinks only for himself.
- Kshatriya-varna: the warrior's dominating gaze of conditional leadership, like a lion who leads his pride so that the lionesses can hunt and bear his children. This is also rajas-guna, as the warrior thinks only for himself.
- Brahmana-varna: the sage's gaze of unconditional leadership, like a cow who provides milk, meant for her calf, generously to the cowherd. She is dependable so the cowherd can always rely on her but she is also independent so while the cowherd needs her, she does not need the

cowherd. This is sattva-guna, as the sage thinks of himself as simply a part of a wider ecosystem, and encourages others to do the same.

Like a dog, I follow unconditionally because I am loyal. Like a deer, I feel safe with the herd.

Like an elephant, I follow the matriarch, as she will find water for me.

Like a lion, I lead the pride because they can hunt for me.

Like a cow, I give my milk to the cowherd without protest, waiting patiently for the cowherd to be generous too.

As Bhairava, Shiva is shown giving shelter to a dog. As Pashupati, Shiva is shown comforting a doe in the palm of his hands. He is also described as wrapped in the hide of an elephant and a lion that he flayed alive. Vishnu is Gopal, associated with the cow.

A yajaman is encouraged to be like Shiva, and give shelter to those who are too frightened to think for themselves. He must also be like Vishnu, encouraging those who are too frightened to think for others to expand their gaze, become more dependable. This is growth.

Every month, Wadhwa would call the heads of his various coaching classes and check how much fees had been collected. But ten years down the road, Wadhwa only checks how many of his students have passed with distinction. The old method meant that the most important department of his company was the sales department; the coaching and quality control department did not matter. With the new method, the passing of students was an indicator of how good the institute was. This demanded that coaches and quality control be first-rate and this made the selling of seats much easier. The shift happened because Wadhwa's gaze shifted from Narayani (share of student's wallet) to Narayan (growth of students). When students began to matter to him genuinely, he made more money than before; but it did not matter. Lakshmi for him was no longer the goal; she was but an indicator. Wadhwa thus moved from vaishya-varna towards brahmana-varna. His leadership is still conditional, but he is moving in the right direction.

Growth is about pursuing thoughts not things

In Hindu mythology, God means what we can become, that is, the acme of human potential. God is visualized either as Shiva, who can give up everything and so is the supreme hermit; or as Vishnu, who can engage with all situations in life with a gentle smile and so is the supreme householder. To be a devotee of God means to try and be like him, in other words invoke the human potential within us.

But Ravan, the rakshasa-king, devotee of Shiva, wants to possess Shiva, rather than be like Shiva. He tries carrying Mount Kailas to his island-kingdom of Lanka and gets crushed under its weight. When pulled out from underneath, he returns home shamefaced, accepting Shiva's superiority, not realizing that the hermit does not seek to be superior. Ravan may be Shiva's devotee but he does not want to see the world as Shiva does. In fact, he assumes like him Shiva also values pecking orders.

By contrast, when Sita offers Hanuman pearls, he bites the pearls to check if Ram is within them. Everyone laughs at this comment: how can Ram who sits on the throne be inside a pearl? "Just as he can be in my heart," says Hanuman, ripping open his chest, revealing Ram within. Hanuman does not care what Ram has, or can give him; he seeks to invoke Ram within himself.

Hanuman seeks to realize his potential, not increase his resources. Ravan, on the other hand, does not believe there is any potential he needs to realize; he is perfect and all he needs is more resources.

Hanuman begins by serving Sugriv out of gratitude to his teacher, the sun-god, Surya, Sugriv's father. He then serves Ram without any expectation or obligation. He moves from vaishya-varna (conditional follower of Sugriv) to brahmana-varna (unconditional leader like Ram). Ravan, on the other hand, slips from being kshatriya-varna (conditional leader of Lanka) to vaishya-varna (conditional follower of Shiva).

It is important to note that Ravan is often called a brahmin, which means he belongs to brahmana-jati. He belongs to a family of priests but chooses to be a king. This does not mean he is of brahmana-varna. In the workplace, we often mistake educational qualifications and institutional pedigree, which is jati, for attitude and potential, which is varna. We may not be able to change our jati, but we can always change our varna.

When asked why many public projects fail, this is the answer a retired civil servant gave, "If two tenders come, the officer will always pass the one at the lower cost. Why? Because then he will not be asked too many questions by his superiors. He knows that the price will be inflated midway through the project when it is impossible to change contractors. But he will keep quiet. Should he choose a better candidate, on qualitative rather than quantitative grounds, he will be pulled up by the audit committee and be forced to answer a lot of questions. So to save himself the trouble, he just accepts the lowest quote, ignoring all qualitative aspects." What the civil servant is saying is that the system encourages rajas-guna (lead or follow so long as it serves you) or tamas-guna (mindlessly follow), not sattva-guna. "Naturally, things are going awry." The servants of the system are turning into Ravans not Hanumans, because upstream and downstream, everyone is only paying attention to things not thoughts, evidence not intent, resources not gaze.

Growth is indicated when we prefer giving than taking

In the story of Krishna, there are two episodes of vastra haran, of women's clothes being removed. In one, which is described in the Bhagavat Puran, Krishna steals the clothes of the milkmaids while they are bathing in the pond. The women are annoyed but not violated. In the other, which is described in the Mahabharat, the Kauravs strip the Pandav queen, Draupadi, of her clothes, in full view of the royal assembly. Draupadi is humiliated and abused.

In the Bhagavat vastra-haran, Krishna is violating the law but the intent is not malicious and the mood is full of mischief. In the Mahabharat vastra-haran, the Kauravs are not violating the law but the intent is malicious and the mood full of rage.

Krishna wants the women to know he appreciates their bodies, in their most natural states, wrinkles and all, without adornment. The Kauravs want to abuse Draupadi while arguing that since she has been gambled away as a slave, they are well within their rights to do whatever they please with her.

In both cases something is being taken but the bhaav is very different. Krishna takes to enable the Other to outgrow the fear that causes embarrassment. The Kauravs take to instil and amplify fear. Krishna seeks to generate trust. The Kauravs seek to establish authority. Krishna grants Saraswati while the Kauravs take Durga.

The yajaman who takes with the desire to dominate and domesticate is not on the path to becoming Vishnu. He will only create rana-bhoomi, not ranga-bhoomi, as he does not include the devata in his world. He wants to control the world of the devata rather than understand it.

Duryodhan dominates Draupadi because he feels she has hurt him. He wants to punish her. In his eyes, he is meting out justice. But he is capable of outgrowing his anger towards her by understanding her reasons for hurting him. The reason is invariably rooted in fear; when this is understood every villain evokes karuna, compassion.

The idea of karuna is an essential thought in Buddhism. When we realize that people do what we consider villainous deeds out of fear, we do not condemn them, or patronize them, but find out in our heart what it is about us that makes them fear us too. Only when we recognize that perhaps we are the cruel parent, or we are perceived as the cruel parent, will we empathize with the Other. The story of Buddha's life is filled with instances where he meets angry beings: from a mad elephant to a murderous serial killer, Angulimala. They calm down before the Buddha because he 'sees' them and understands where they are coming from. They are not condemned for their behaviour; that their belief springs from fear is understood.

Karuna demands the expanding of the mind. This is visualized as the lotus. Hence Buddha is often shown holding a lotus, a gesture known as Padmapani, he who held the lotus. Sometimes the goddess Tara, embodiment of pragna, or wisdom, holds the lotus.

In every conversation, Sunil wants to dominate. He wants to come across as the alpha. He must know more than the Other. He must know things before the Other. He is constantly seeking Durga every time he dismisses those before him. The day he starts to listen, allows people to express themselves, appreciates their point of view, feels comfortable giving rather than receiving Durga, he will have grown. He will be more Vishnu, fountainhead of security, and more people will be attracted to him.

Growth happens when more people can depend on us

In the Ramayan, Lakshman is the obedient and loyal younger brother of Ram, following him wherever he goes, doing whatever he is told to do. One day, Ram tells Lakshman, "I want solitude so I am shutting the door of my chambers. Do not let anyone in. Kill anyone who tries to open it." Lakshman swears to do so.

No sooner is the door shut than Rishi Durvasa, renowned for his temper, demands a meeting with Ram. Lakshman tries to explain the situation. "I don't care," says an impatient and enraged Durvasa, "If I don't see the king of Ayodhya this very minute I shall curse his kingdom with drought and misfortune." At that moment Lakshmana wonders what matters more: his promise to his brother, or the safety of Ayodhya? What decision must he take? Must he be karya-karta or yajaman?

Lakshman concludes that Ayodhya is more important and so opens the door to announce Durvasa. But when he turns around there is no sign of Durvasa. And Ram says, "I am glad you finally disobeyed me and decided Ayodhya matters more than Ram."

The tryst with Durvasa makes Lakshman ask the fundamental question, "For whom are you doing what you are doing?" Lakshman realizes in his yagna, all his life, Ram was the only devata. But with this decision, he has made all of Ayodhya his devata. His gaze has expanded. Until then only Ram could depend on him. Now all of Ayodhya can depend on him.

Lakshman realizes that obedience is neither good nor bad. What matters is the reason behind the obedience, the belief behind behaviour. Is it rooted in fear or is it rooted in wisdom? Does he obey to ensure self-preservation, self-propagation and self-actualization or because he cares for the Other? A yagna is truly successful when the svaha helps both devata and the yajaman outgrow dependence.

When Shailesh moves, he takes his team with him. So everyone knows when Shailesh resigns from a company, six more people will go. Shailesh thinks of this as his great strength. He has a power team that can change the fortunes of a company. He does not realize this is also his weakness. He does not see new talent and new capabilities and capacities. His team is his comfort zone and he is assuming they will be strong and smart enough for any situation. Will they be as successful in a new situation, in a new market, when economic realities change, when resources are scarce, when clients demand different things? Shailesh will grow only when he is able to expand his team, include new people, allow people to move out, work on their own. He is growing too dependent on his team and they are too dependent on him. It is time for him to become more independent, to become dependable to others.

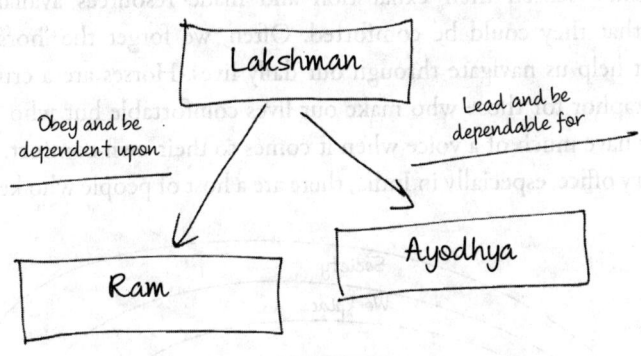

Growth happens when even the insignificant become significant

For eighteen days, the Kauravs and the Pandavs fight on the plains of Kurukshetra. Hundreds of soldiers are killed on either side. In the middle of the war, Krishna tells Arjun, "We have to stop. The horses are tired. They need to rest and be refreshed. Shoot your arrow into the ground and bring out some water so that I can bathe and water the horses. Keep the enemy at bay with a volley of arrows while I do so." Arjun does as instructed. Refreshed, the horses pull the chariot with renewed vigour.

The horses pulling Arjun's chariot did not ask to be refreshed. Krishna sensed their exhaustion and made resources available so that they could be comforted. Often, we forget the 'horses' that help us navigate through our daily lives. Horses are a crude metaphor for those who make our lives comfortable but who do not have much of a voice when it comes to their own comfort. In every office, especially in India, there are a host of people who keep

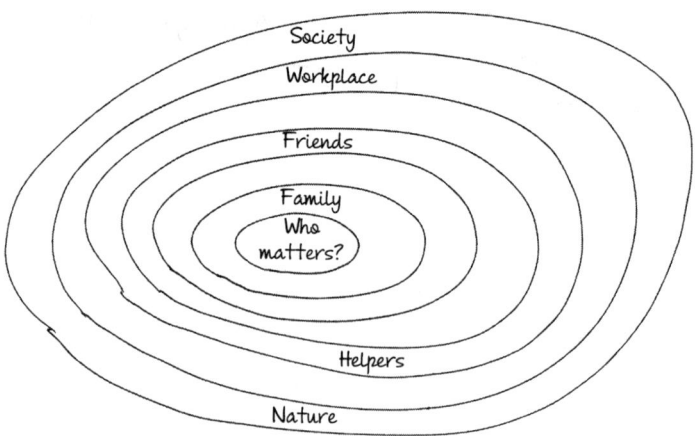

the office running—the office boy, canteen boy, security guard, drivers, peons, and so on. This is the silent support staff. They take care of the 'little things' that enable us to achieve the 'big things'. A simple study of how organizations treat this silent support staff is an indicator of leadership empathy.

Randhir drives his boss to work every day negotiating heavy highway traffic for over two hours to and fro. His boss, Mr Chaudhary, is a partner in a large consulting firm that is responsible for over fifty high net worth clients. This means a lot of travel both in the city and outside, which means many trips to the airport early in the morning and late at night. This also means travelling from meetings from one end of the city to another and short trips to satellite cities. Randhir is frustrated. His boss does not know that he lives in a shantytown an hour away from Mr Chaudhary's swanky apartment block. To travel to his place of work, he needs to take a bus or an auto. These are not easily available early in the morning or late at night. His travel allowance is insufficient to take care of this. When he raised this issue with Mr Chaudhary, he was told, "This is what the company policy says you should be paid." Randhir does not understand policy. He serves Mr Chaudhary, not the company. But Mr Chaudhary does not see it that way. And then there are Sundays when Mr Chaudhary visits his farmhouse with his wife and children. No holidays for Randhir. "His family is in the village so why does he need a holiday?" Often there is no parking space at places where Mr Chaudhary has meetings. At times, there are parking spaces but no amenities for drivers—no place to rest and no bathrooms. "You cannot eat in the car; I do not like the smell," says Mr Chaudhary, who also disables the music system when he leaves the car "so that he does not waste the battery." And when Mr Chaudhary got a huge 40 per cent bonus over and above his two crore rupee CTC, he very generously gave Randhir a 500 rupee hike. "I am being fair. That's more than the drivers of others got. I don't want to disrupt the driver market."

The Talent Sutra

Growth happens when we include those whom we once excluded

In the Mahabharat, during the game of dice, Yudhishtir gambles away his kingdom and then starts wagering his brothers. He begins with the twins, Nakul and Sahadev, and then gambles away Bhim and Arjun, then himself and finally, their common wife, Draupadi.

Later, during his forest exile, his brothers drink water from a forbidden pond and all die. The guardian of the pond, a stork, offers to resurrect to life one of the four brothers. Yudhishtir asks for Nakul to be resurrected. "Why not mighty Bhim or the archer Arjun?" asks the stork. To this Yudhishtir replies, "Because Nakul is the son of Madri, my father's second wife. If I, son of Kunti, first wife of my father, Pandu, am alive, surely a son of Madri needs to survive too. When Madri died, Kunti promised to take care of her children. I have to uphold my mother's promise."

Thus we see a transformation in Yudhishtir. The stepbrother who is the first to be gambled away is also the first to be resurrected. He, who was excluded before, and hence dispensable, has been included. The king who sacrificed the least fit person now helps the most helpless. Yudhishtir's gaze has thus expanded from taking care of himself to taking care of others. His mind has expanded and he has risen in varna. He has become more dependable. He has grown.

At a party, Karan met Mansoor, who had unceremoniously fired him years ago. He found himself caught up in a dilemma. Should he speak to Mansoor, relive those ugly memories? Should he discreetly avoid eye contact? Suddenly, Mansoor waved to him with a smile and asked him to join the group he was with. "This is Karan," he said, "We worked together a long time ago." He did not mentioning the firing or the unpleasantness of the past. He had moved on in his mind, and made no attempt to justify his action or apologize. Karan, who was once excluded, suddenly felt included. It felt good.

Growth happens when we stop seeing people as villains

In the final chapter of the Mahabharat, Yudhishtir renounces his kingdom and passes on his crown to his grandson Parikshit and sets out for the forest. His wife and brothers follow him. As they are climbing the mountains, they start falling into the deep ravine below, one by one. Yudhishtir does not turn around to help them, "Because," he says, "I have renounced everything."

When he is alone, with no one but a dog for company, Indra opens the gates of Amravati and lets him in. "Dogs are inauspicious," says Indra, "This dog cannot come in." Yudhishtir refuses to enter Amravati without the dog because the dog has been his one true companion. Indra relents.

Inside Amravati, Yudhishtir finds the Kauravs enjoying the joys of paradise. "How can that be?" asks Yudhishtir angrily, "If these warmongering villains can be allowed here, surely my brothers should be allowed here too. Where are they?"

At this point Indra says, "You demand that your unconditional follower enter paradise with you, but you are unwilling to share paradise unconditionally with those who have already been punished for their crimes. When will you forgive them, Yudhishtir? How long will you hold on to your anger? Can Swarga be yours unless you lead unconditionally?"

Inclusion means not just allowing those who follow you into paradise, but also making room for those who reject and oppose you. This is brahmana-varna.

Vimla is happy with herself. There was a time she would find disorganized people very irritating. She would try to correct them. And punish them if they resisted. Over the years, as she rose to head the audit department, she realized that different people function differently. That it was perfectly fine to not be as organized as she herself was, or to be differently organized. She no longer mocks those who are different. She includes them. She has grown.

Growth happens when we seek to uplift the Other

The word dharma has often been translated as ethics, morality, righteousness and goodness. These English words are rooted in the notion of objectivity. But dharma is not an objective concept. It is a subjective concept based on gaze.

Depending on our varna, we will see dharma differently. For the shudra, it is doing what the master tells him to do. For the vaishya, it is doing what he feels is right. For the kshatriya, it is doing what he feels is right for all. For the brahman, it is realizing that each one is right in his own way, but each one can be more right, by expanding his gaze. As our gaze expands, our varna changes and so does dharma.

Dharma is about realizing our potential. While all other creatures grow at the cost of others (plants feed on minerals, animals feed on plants and other animals), humans can grow by helping others grow. This is not sacrifice. This is not selflessness. This is making the yajaman's growth an outcome of the devata's growth. This is best demonstrated in the ritual that takes place during Nanda Utsav.

Every year, during the festival of Nanda Utsav, pots of butter are hung from great heights and human pyramids are formed to climb to the pot, commemorating how Krishna would steal butter from the milkmaids of Gokul and Vrindavan that was kept out of his reach when he was a child. In this exercise, the most crucial stage is the one in which people in the lowermost tier, who sit while the pyramid is being set up, have to stand up. Only when they stand, balancing the entire pyramid on their shoulders does Krishna get the butter. In their growth lies Krishna's success.

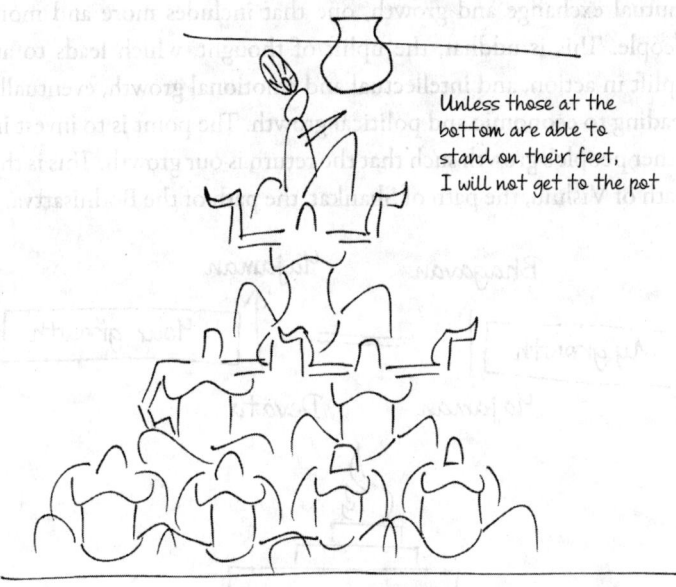

True expansion happens when I grow because you grow. When only I grow, it is selfish. When only you grow, it is selfless. Only plants and animals are allowed to be selfish, as they do not have the capacity to imagine, hence empathize. Only minerals and inanimate objects can be truly selfless.

In sanatan, only the digambar shramana, or the naked, wise sage can be truly selfless. Only he has no fear and can walk around without food, shelter or clothing, comfortable as he is. That is why monks were associated with forests, not social organizations, never allowed to stay or settle in a single place. Around Shiva, there are only snow-capped mountains where no life can thrive. It is good for the individual but not for those who are dependent on him.

For society, we need neither selfishness nor selflessness. We need a connection with the ecosystem. We need a method of mutual exchange and growth, one that includes more and more people. This is uddhar, the uplift of thought, which leads to an uplift in action, and intellectual and emotional growth, eventually leading to economic and political growth. The point is to invest in other people's growth such that the return is our growth. This is the path of Vishnu, the path of Shankar, the path of the Bodhisattva.

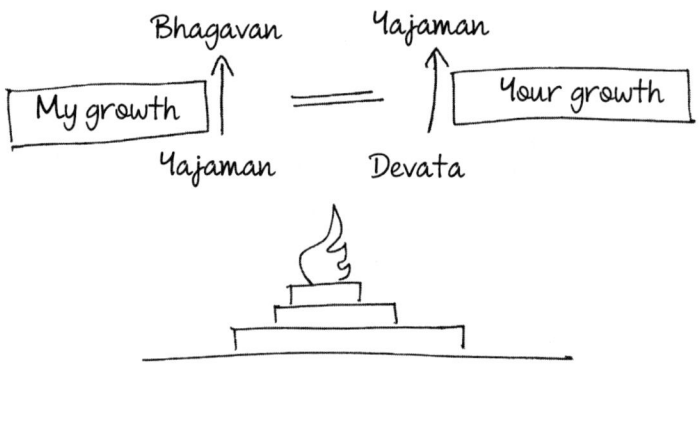

When Vikram took over as the CEO, he called the head of his human resource department and said he wanted to redesign job descriptions. He wanted financial goals to be the primary objective of executives. He wanted customer satisfaction and employee engagement to be the primary objective of junior managers. He wanted talent management to be the primary objective of senior managers. "As you climb the ladder, you cannot be paying attention to the same thing the same way," states Vikram.

Inclusion

It is easier to teach than to learn. It is easier to instruct than to let people be. It is easier to focus on things than thoughts. It is easier to expand our mind than get others to expand their minds. Wisdom is having the faith and patience to create an ecosystem where the mind-lotus can bloom at its own pace, on its own terms.

More yajamans are needed as an organization grows

At first, the yagna is small and simple. As the yagna progresses into a sattra and more fires are lit, specializations arise. Those who chant hymns and make offerings sit close to the fire. Those who protect the enclosure stand a little beyond. Those who get the firewood, mould the bricks, bake the pots, weave the cloth, tend to the cows and grow the crops, visit the enclosure only occasionally. Those who clean the enclosure are never seen as they emerge only when everyone has left.

Over time, those closest to the fire get the most attention and receive the most value while those who are further away and rarely seen, get the least attention and least value. This is because, often, though the yagna grows in size, the yajaman's gaze does not. This gives rise to the caste system where people are classified for the value placed on their measurable contribution (jati). Sanskriti becomes no different from prakriti where the dictum of survival of the fittest applies—the powerful thrive on resources and the less valued perish.

But humans are not animals. When Brahma at the top behaves like Gandhari, those at the bottom transform into Duryodhan, or even Ravan; at first subversive, but eventually defiant. When those at the top of the pyramid behave like devas and yakshas, those at the bottom will turn into asuras and rakshasas. Conflict rages. The sea rises. Pralay is imminent. All because Brahma was being stubborn and refused to see.

That is why in India the divine gaze is scattered and distributed through a variety of deities: gods who look after individuals (ishta-devata); gods who look after the household (griha-devata); gods who look after the village (grama-devata); gods who look after the city (nagar-devata); gods who look after the forest (vana-devata); and gods who look after communities (kula-devata).

These are not diminutive replicas of the distant bhagavan. Rather, each of these deities has an individual personality, a local flavour. The deities help in expanding and extending the gaze of the common bhagavan. Despite different roles, responsibilities and contributions, none of them feels inferior or superior; everyone feels revered.

Similarly, to create an organization where everyone feels they matter, it is important to extend the central gaze to the periphery, much like the hub-and-spoke model of supply chains which decentralized decision-making so that every local market got attention from a local office, and did not rely on the gaze of the central office. However, this can only work when the head of the local office is as much of a deity in his or her own right and not subordinate to the deity in the central office.

Every deity takes ownership and acts locally keeping in mind global needs, sensitive to the internal organizational ecosystem as well as external market conditions. It is the yajaman's responsibility to create more Vishnus who know how to descend (avatarana) and to uplift (uddhar) those around them. Otherwise he will end up creating frightened sons of Brahma who think only of themselves and forget that a yagna is an exchange.

When he had only one office and thirty people serving clients, Sandeep could make everyone in his team feel included. Now that he's been promoted, he is a distant god; no one connects with him. They rarely see him except at the annual town hall meetings where he speaks, but never listens. Sandeep's managers feel they are merely his handmaidens and his messengers, with no power or say in local matters. Naturally, the energy that once buzzed around Sandeep is restricted to the corporate office. In zonal, regional and local offices, there is just process, tasks and targets, very little proactivity or enthusiasm.

The yajaman has to turn devatas into yajamans

The sage Agastya performed tapasya and wanted to have nothing to do with society. But he was tormented all night by dreams of his ancestors who begged him to father a child. "Just as we gave you life, you have to give someone else life." This is Pitr-rin, one's debt to one's ancestors: one is not allowed to die unless one leaves behind a life on earth.

Thus every yajaman is obliged to create another yajaman to replace him. This makes talent creation an obligation. Talent management is not merely the passing on of knowledge and skills; it is the expanding of the gaze of the next generation of managers. It is the responsibility of those upstream to help those downstream see the world as they do.

A new manager can be equated to the many images of gods and goddesses sold in the market; they are not worshipped until

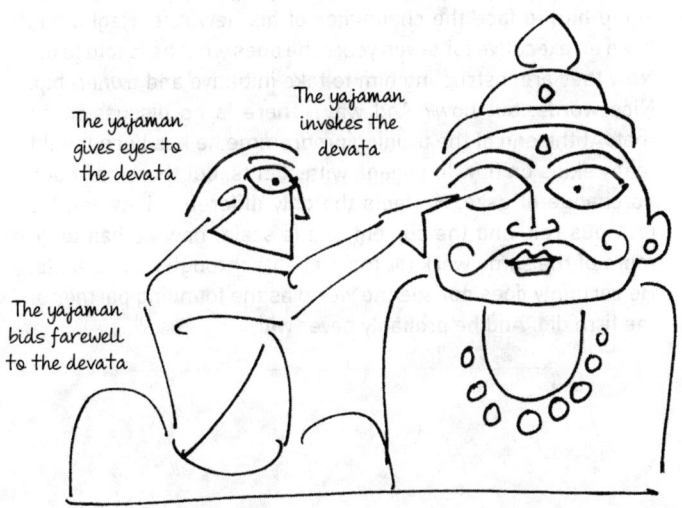

the ritual of prana-prathistha or the giving of life. This involves chakshu-daan, the granting of eyes, whereby the image becomes sentient and sensitive to the human condition, hence a deity. The yajaman thus gives eyes to the devata, helps the Other see what he can see. This is the essence of talent management.

A yajaman can be self-created, self-motivated, swayambhu. Or he may be created by another yajaman. Daksha sees talent development as an obligation and converts it into a process, a series of ritual steps. Indra sees talent management as a burden; he is even threatened by the talent. Vishnu sees talent management as an opportunity to help himself: for by helping someone else grow, we grow ourselves. By making another person dependable, the yajaman liberates himself from current responsibilities so that he can take on new responsibilities.

Raghu is a consultant in a large auditing firm. He has been made a manager with client-facing responsibilities. And he has been asked to attend a training programme designed to equip him to face the challenges of his new role. Raghu has been an executive for seven years; he does what he is told to do. Now they are instructing him to take initiative and ownership. Nice words, but how? And why? There is no discussion on that. At the end of the training programme he has been taught many skills on how to engage with clients, but there has been no change of gaze. He feels the only difference between his previous role and the current one is scale: now he has to do more of the same work for more clients through more people. He certainly does not see the world as the founding partner of the firm did. And he probably never will.

Creating talent enables us to grow

Vedic scriptures divide life into four phases: in the first phase we are students (brahmachari); in the second, we are householders (grihasthi); in the third, we retire (vanaprasthi); in the fourth, we renounce the world and retreat to the forest (sanyasi). The person who retires educates the student before he is allowed to renounce the world for the householder is too busy earning a livelihood for his family. Thus while grihasthi is focused on wealth generation, the vanaprasthi and the brahmachari are involved in knowledge transmission.

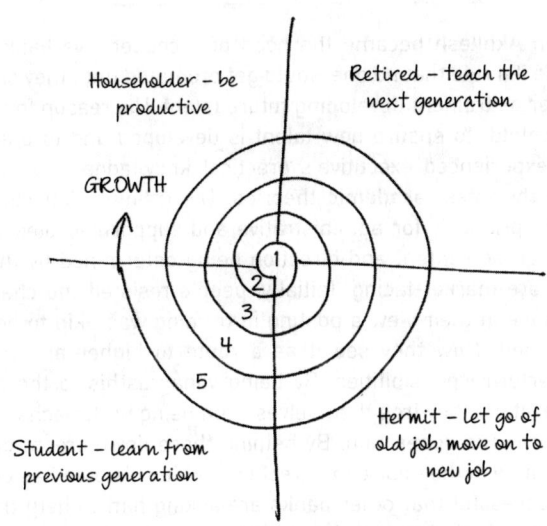

Our time in a particular job, or in a role, can be seen as a lifetime. We are born when we get a job and we die when we leave that job. In every job, there is a learning phase and a productive phase, and eventually a time to move on. In between there is boredom and frustration. The monotony of the job gets to us. The executive wants to be manager and the manager wants to be director.

This is when it is time to retire. We seek new opportunities, different opportunities or greater responsibilities, either in the same organization or another. We seek the death of our current job and rebirth in another. In other words, we seek growth.

But to grow into the next job, we have to create talent from someone downstream who will replace us and make ourselves available to someone upstream, who by helping us grow enables us to move on to the next phase of our career.

When Akhilesh became the head of a cooperative bank, he made it a rule that no one would get promoted until they spent a year as trainers developing future talent. His reason for this is twofold: to ensure new talent is developed and to ensure the experienced executive's practical knowledge is updated with the latest academic theories. His training department exists primarily for administrative and supportive roles with the course content and direction being determined by those who are market-facing. Initially, people resisted the change because in their view a posting in training was akin to being sidelined. Now they see it as a route to higher and more powerful responsibilities. By being vanaprasthis to the next generation, they free themselves from being brahmacharis to the previous generation. By helping those downstream grow they grow in the upstream direction. Akhilesh's plan has been so successful that other banks are asking him to help them set up a similar system. It is not about creating a system: it is about giving attention to what matters.

We seek to inherit things, not thoughts

At the end of the war at Kurukshetra, as the victorious Pandavs are about to assume control of Hastinapur after vanquishing the Kauravs, Krishna advises them to talk to Bhisma, their granduncle, who lies mortally wounded on the battlefield. As the result of a blessing, death will elude him for some time. "Make him talk until his last breath. Ask him questions. He has a lot to tell and you have a lot to learn," says Krishna.

Sure enough, when prompted, the dying Bhisma spends hours discussing various topics: history, geography, politics, economics, management, war, ethics, morality, sex, astronomy, metaphysics and philosophy. Bhisma's discourse is captured in the Shanti Parva (discussions on peace) and Anushasan Parva (discussions on discipline) that make up a quarter of the Mahabharat. After listening to their grandsire, the Pandavs have a better understanding of the world, and this makes them better kings.

The Pandavs need Krishna's prompting to seek knowledge from Bhisma. They do not need this prompting to sit on the throne or wear the crown. Like plants and animals, we are naturally drawn to Lakshmi and not Saraswati. We have not yet got used to what it means to be human. Tapping our human potential is not our top priority. We are convinced we have already realized it. Hence the focus on growing what we have rather than who we are.

Gyansingh watches in dismay as his children fight over the property and business. For years, he insisted they work with him. He wanted them to learn the tricks of the business, but they sat with him only out of a sense of duty. He sensed they did not think they had much to learn. They had their degrees from great colleges and so assumed they knew everything. All they wanted from Gyansingh was power and control. They see him as the source of Lakshmi and Durga not Saraswati.

Being a yajaman is about gaze, not skills

When Vishnu descends as Parashuram, he has three students: Bhisma, Drona and Karna. When he descends as Krishna, he gets all three killed on the battlefield of Kurukshetra, for they had failed him as students.

All three learnt the art of warfare from Parashuram and became great warriors. The purpose of all Vishnu's avatars is to establish dharma. Dharma is not about skill; it is about gaze. None of these students expanded their gaze; their gaze was focused on their own desires and anxieties and fears and hence they ended up leading the Kaurav army, much to Vishnu's dismay.

Every Brahma focuses on understanding prakriti so that he can control the outer world. Few focus on understanding purush so that they can develop their inner world. Sharda does not matter as much as Vidyalakshmi.

Since every Brahma is convinced that his gaze is perfect, he focuses on domesticating the world around him with rules. But for humans, dharma is about expanding the gaze. When the gaze expands the futility of trying to dominate those around us or domesticating them with rules is revealed.

Parmesh, the head of the training department in a public sector company, has come to the conclusion that most people see promotions as a chance to wield authority and dominate those around them. They see being bossy as a perk. They do not see promotions as enabling them to see the organization, the market and themselves differently. This belief stops them from acquiring new knowledge and skills, or paying attention to the gaze of seniors. They see training simply as a way by which the organization domesticates talent. That is why, while they court promotions, they resist coming to training programmes; they already know what they need to know. What they do not know they expect their juniors to know.

Questions teach us, not answers

Students can be classified as the five Pandavs: Yudhishtir, Bhim, Arjun, Nakul and Sahadev.

- Yudhishtir, as king, expects others to know the answers.
- Bhim, a man of strength, prefers to do rather than think.
- Arjun, as an archer, sees questions as arrows shot at him and deflects them by asking counter questions. He is not interested in the answer.
- Nakul, the handsome one, is not capable of thought.
- Sahadev is the wise one who never speaks but is constantly thinking and analyzing. When asked a question, he is provoked into thought and comes up with an intelligent answer. If not asked a question, he stays silent.

A teacher who wants to invoke Narayan in his students follows the Sahadev-method of teaching: he asks questions and does not give answers. The teacher is not obliged to know the answer. The questions are meant to provoke thought, create emotional turmoil and inspire the student to find the answer. For the answers benefit the student, no one else. If the student refuses to find the answer, it is his loss, not the teacher's.

In the *Kathasaritsagar*, Vetal makes Vikramaditya wiser by asking him questions. The crematorium where the Vetal lives is the training room, where the past is processed for wisdom that can be applied in the future. Vikramaditya has to come to the Vetal if he wishes to serve his kingdom better. He has to come and then return. If Vikramaditya chose not to go to the crematorium or answer any question, it would be his loss not the Vetal's who is already dead.

The Vetal must never go to Vikramaditya's kingdom, for he will end up haunting the land of the living.

When Lydia was appointed the head of the learning and development wing, she laid down some ground rules. Trainers were told not to herd participants into training rooms: they were free to come and go as they pleased. Learning was their responsibility, not the trainers'. They were not children who had to be disciplined. There was very little instruction on the part of the trainers; there were only questions asked and participants were encouraged to answer and analyse the reasons for the answers. Case studies were prepared using the knowledge of the organization itself. Sales, marketing, production, logistics and accounts officers were videofilmed and asked to present the common problems they faced and issues they expected to resolve so that everyone could share their thoughts on these. The focus was on practical work rather than theory, active answering rather than passive listening. Lydia put up a notice at the entrance stating, "Unless you speak we are not sure if you have learned anything."

We resist advice and instructions

While King Virata of Matsya was away chasing the king of Trigarta, who had stolen his cows, the Kaurav army took advantage of his absence and attacked the city. There was no one around to defend the city except the women and children. Everyone was frightened. "Do not worry, I will protect you," said the confident young prince, Uttar.

A eunuch called Brihanalla who taught dancing to the princess warned the prince that the Kauravs were a mighty force not to be taken lightly and that no single warrior could defeat them, except maybe Arjun. Uttar did not take too kindly to this comment. He admonished Brihanalla. "Know your place in the palace," he roared. Brihanalla apologized immediately. Unfortunately for the prince, there were no charioteers left in the city. "What do I do now? How can I ride into battle without a charioteer?" he whined. Brihanalla offered him his services, claiming to have some experience in charioteering. Though not happy to have a eunuch as his charioteer, the pompous prince, armed with a bow, rode out with Brihanalla to face the Kauravs in battle, cheered on by the palace women. When Uttar entered the battlefield and saw the enemy before him, he trembled in fear. Before him were great warriors, archers and swordsmen on horses, elephants and chariots. In a panic, Uttar jumped off the chariot and began running back towards the city. The Kauravs roared with laughter, further humiliating the embarrassed prince.

The eunuch-charioteer then turned the chariot around, chased the prince, caught up with him and drove him out of the battlefield into a nearby forest where she revealed that she was no eunuch but Arjun, the great archer, in disguise. "I will not tell your father about your cowardice but you must promise not tell anyone who I really am," said Brihanalla. An awestruck Uttar agreed.

And so Brihanalla pushed back the enemy and Uttar returned to a hero's welcome. But the prince was not carried away by the praise; he knew the truth about himself. He was grateful to Arjun for revealing to him the truth about his martial abilities, without taking away his dignity.

This story from the Virata Parva of the Mahabharat provides an important lesson in mentoring. Arjun is Uttar's mentor. Uttar imagines his capability and is ignorant about the true identity of his eunuch-charioteer until he is faced with a crisis. Arjun is mature enough not to humiliate the young, inexperienced prince, focusing instead on his growth. Students do not like being told what they can and cannot do. They need to discover it for themselves. Crisis usually helps.

When Dilip came back from business school with a business idea, his uncle Naresh agreed to fund him. "But it will not work," shouted Dilip's father, Mahesh. "I know," said Naresh, "He is young and wilful and will not listen to us. He has to figure it out himself. Besides, we could be wrong. If he succeeds with the money I give him we all will benefit. If he loses, he will come back a seasoned, battle-scarred businessman."

The Talent Sutra

Discourses never transform us

Just before the battle of Kurukshetra is about to begin, Arjun loses his nerve. He suddenly realizes the enormity of the situation before him. He is about to kill his kith and kin for a piece of property. He is consumed by guilt and shame. He throws his bow down and refuses to fight. This is when Krishna reveals to him the secret of life in a song thereafter known as the Bhagavad Gita. Enlightened by the wisdom, Arjun picks up his bow and prepares to fight. Or so we are told.

During the course of the war, Arjun loses his nerve time and time again. Krishna has to goad him on to kill Bhisma, the first commander of the Kaurav army. He is then reluctant to kill his teacher, Drona. He is shattered when his son Abhimanyu is killed. He finds it hard to kill the unarmed Karna even when Krishna advises him to. He is hardly the wise warrior, displaying equanimity in the middle of crisis.

We would like to believe that a training programme will transform people forever but it does not. An agreement with a professor does not mean one has understood the subject. What the professor says is smriti—the outer voice that can be spoken, but is not necessarily heard. What is ultimately heard is shruti—our inner voice, which is heard but can never be spoken.

Haider has attended many leadership-training workshops. At the end of each workshop he feels charged and motivated. When it comes to actually leading people though he fails miserably. No one listens to him. Then one day, he asks himself, "Why should people follow me? What am I offering that makes me attractive?" As he ponders over the question, his understanding of himself and those around him improves.

He is more interested in playing boss he realizes and not really in taking people along with him. Moreover, he is only interested in his goals with no interest in the goals of others. This stems from his fear of being ignored. The more he introspects, the more the frameworks he's learned in the classroom start making sense. The smriti becomes shruti. And the penny drops.

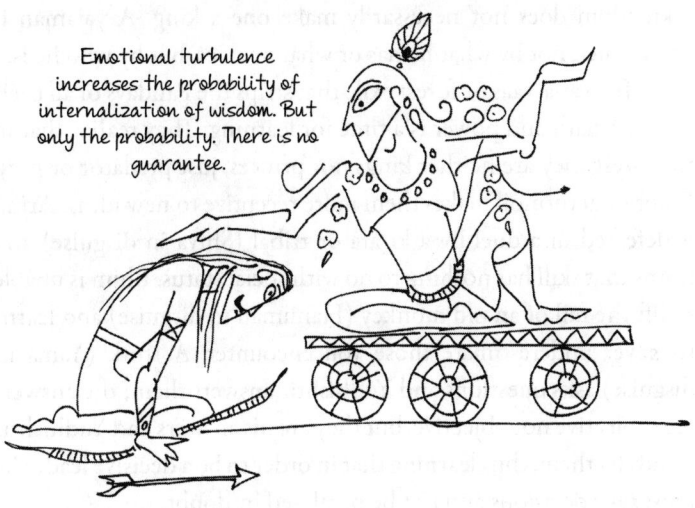

Emotional turbulence increases the probability of internalization of wisdom. But only the probability. There is no guarantee.

Crisis increases the chances of learning

As Ram, Vishnu is king in the Ramayan, but as Krishna, he is kingmaker in the Mahabharat. With Krishna's help the Pandavs built the city of Indraprastha. But as soon as he is gone, the Pandavs gamble this kingdom away. Thus they learn that having a kingdom does not necessarily make one a king. A yajaman is determined not by what he has or what he does, but by who he is.

The vana-vaas or forest exile that strips the Pandavs of all their status, wealth and power is a time for learning. They realize that in the forest they are neither kings nor princes, just predator or prey. Emotional turmoil makes them more receptive to new ideas. Arjun is defeated in a duel by a kirata or tribal (Shiva in disguise) and learns that skill has nothing to do with social status. Bhim is unable to lift the tail of an old monkey (Hanuman in disguise) and learns to never underestimate those you encounter. A stork (Yama in disguise) asks questions and Yudhishtir answers them; the answers are subjective not objective, but they are his answers and Yudhishtir stands by them, thus learning that in order to be a decisive leader he must take decisions and not be paralysed by doubt.

In their final year of exile, the Pandavs, former kings, live in another king's palace disguised as servants. This is not humiliation but rather darshan: they are seeing how the world looks from the bottom of the pyramid.

At the end of the exile, Krishna goes to the Kauravs to negotiate peace. The point is not to punish the villain but to invoke the Narayan in him so that he realizes the value of coexistence and generosity. Unfortunately, Duryodhan refuses to part with even a 'needlepoint of land'. This territorial behaviour makes Duryodhan an animal, a pack leader not a yajaman. Since he behaves like a beast he needs to be killed by any means. Krishna declares war.

The final lesson is imparted during the war itself. What is the goal of the war: to win back the kingdom or to expand the gaze? The war, like any other, has terrible consequences that the Pandavs have to face. They have to kill their elder (Bhisma), teacher (Drona), brother (Karna) and suffer the deaths of their own children. They learn the cost of being territorial.

In the forest, the varna of the Pandavs changes. They are no longer conditional leaders. They become unconditional leaders who conduct the yagna not to dominate or domesticate the devatas for their own benefit, but to uplift them for everyone's benefit. In the war, this growth in varna is severely tested.

During interviews, Arvind only asks candidates to talk about their failures. He wants to see how they reacted in adverse situations. Did they bemoan the loss of Lakshmi and Durga, or did they gain Saraswati to enable future success? As far as Arvind is concerned, the tathastu of Saraswati is most available during vana-vaas when we feel we have failed in the system and find ourselves out in the wilderness with no direction or purpose.

Power play underlies the process of teaching

When Vishnu approaches Bali as the child Vaman and asks for three paces of land, it is in the third step that he turns into a giant. With the first two paces he covers all that Bali possessed. "Now where do I place my foot to claim my third pace?" he asks. Bali bows and offers his head. Vishnu shoves him to Patala, the nether regions where asuras belong.

Why does Vaman turn from dwarf into giant? Is it to dominate Bali and show him who the alpha is? Is it to domesticate Bali and compel him to respect cosmic rules? Or is it to make Bali open his eyes: make him realize that the answer to life's problem is not in Narayani (the availability of resources), symbolized by the gift of three paces of land, but in Narayan (the human potential), symbolized by the dwarf's ability to become a giant?

The answer rests with Bali: how does he receive Vaman's action, Vaman's intention notwithstanding? Bali's bowing could be indicative of his surrender to Vishnu, his submission to the rules, or a genuine expression of gratitude following the expansion of his mind. Only he knows.

Sandeep was a successful businessman who insisted that his son Vikas use public transport till he finished college. He wanted his son to learn the realities of life, learn that wealth and power are privileges and not entitlements. Unfortunately, Vikas does not see things that way. His friends would tease him every time they saw him at the bus stop; their parents had provided them with drivers and cars. Vikas felt his father was old-fashioned and stingy. Sandeep never understood why there was so much a distance in his relationship with Vikas.

To teach, we have to learn to let go

While searching for Sita's whereabouts Hanuman sets aflame the city of Lanka of his own volition. This displeased Ram as he had no desire to hurt the residents of Lanka for the crime of their king. Not wanting to displease Ram ever again, Hanuman swore never to take any decision without consulting Ram.

This absolute obedience became so intense that it alarmed Jambuvan, the wise bear, who also served in the army of animals raised by Ram to defeat Ravan and liberate Sita. When Hanuman was being given instructions on how to find the Sanjivani herb that could save Lakshman from certain death after being injured in battle, Jambuvan told Ram, "Make sure to tell him clearly that he has to come back with the herb after he's found it. Otherwise, he will find the herb and simply wait by the mountain in complete compliance." This was not good, Ram realized. The situation had to be rectified.

As is related in the Adbhut Ramayan, during the course of the war, Ravan's cousin Mahiravan, a sorcerer, managed to abduct both Ram and Lakshman and took them to Patala. Only Hanuman had the intellectual and physical prowess to rescue them. He had to rely on his own wits, as there was no Ram around to instruct him. He was on his own. Jambuvan realized this situation was of Ram's own making. Hanuman was being forced to rise to the challenge.

At one point during the rescue mission, Hanuman had to simultaneously blow out five lamps located in five corners of Patala. He solved this problem by sprouting four extra heads: that of a boar, an eagle, a lion and a horse. With these five heads he could blow out the five lamps easily. Eventually, Hanuman succeeded in rescuing Ram. He had been transformed from an obedient servant to an astute, independent decision maker. He had been transformed from being a Ram-bhakt to Mahavir, from god to God, worthy of veneration in his own right. Ram had thus created a leader.

A time comes in every leader's life when he has to create leaders around him. This involves making one's team members competent enough to take independent decisions. This is not easy, as every decision has consequences, not all of which are acceptable to a leader. It demands tremendous restraint and maturity on a leader's part to not intervene and change the decision taken by a junior.

Hanuman's decision to burn Lanka displeased Ram. And so after that, Hanuman stopped taking decisions. To rectify the damage done, Ram had to remove himself from the scene so that Hanuman could rediscover his decision making abilities. A leader need not agree with a junior's decision. They are two different people and so may not see the same situation in the same way. But to imagine that a subordinate will think just like them, is many a leader's folly.

Sanjeev's brilliant decision making abilities have resulted in his becoming a partner in a consulting firm at a very young age. Now he has to nurture his managers and nudge them to take on more responsibilities. One of his managers, Sebastian, decided to follow up on the status of a business proposal with a client on his own. "Why did you do that?" shouted Sanjeev, "It could put them off." Another time, Sebastian gave a half-day's leave to a management trainee who was feeling unwell. "Why did you do that?" screamed Sanjeev, "There is so much work to do." After this, not wanting to upset his boss further, Sebastian stopped taking decisions independently. He only did what Sanjeev told him to do. During appraisals, Sanjeev said, "You need to be more proactive," much to Sebastian's astonishment and irritation. As a result of his own actions, Sanjeev is surrounded by obedient followers and not leaders.

Only when teachers are willing to learn does growth happen

Shiva is self-contained. So he has no desire to open his eyes to the world. With great difficulty, Gauri makes him open his eyes. She has questions that only he can answer. Shiva reveals why thoughts matter over things, and gaze over skills. As Gauri clarifies her doubts, Shiva begins to appreciate the fear that prevents a Brahma from letting go of things and skills, of all things tangible, of his limited worldview. The conversation provokes empathy in Shiva, transforming him into Shankar-Shambhu, the benevolent one.

Education and learning tend to be linear. In education, the burden of teaching rests with the teacher. In learning, the burden shifts to the student. Both education and learning can be made cyclical, especially in business, when the trainer and the mentor gives Vidyalakshmi and gets Sharda in return, even without the

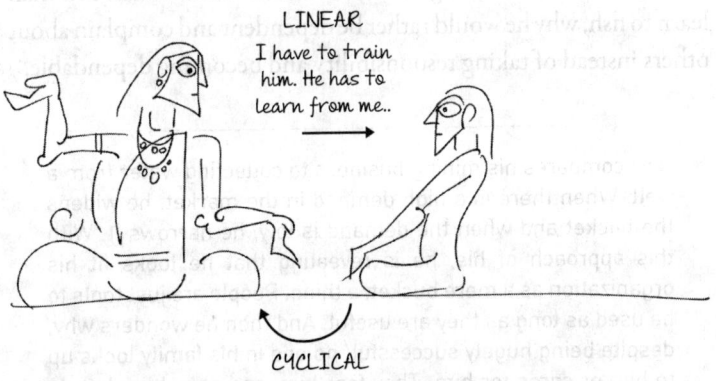

LINEAR
I have to train him. He has to learn from me..

CYCLICAL
I discover the essence of communication, what works and what does not work, why something works and why something does not. This learning makes me less impatient and more wise.

active participation of the participant. The yajaman can learn from the devata even if the devata refuses to learn from the yajaman. The yajaman can learn what makes a devata curious and eager for knowledge and what stops him from being curious and eager. This learning reveals to him the human condition, widens his gaze, makes him a more dependable and understanding yajaman.

In business, it is easy to get cynical about people's ability to learn and think that the only way to get work done is by dominating or domesticating others with rules and systems, by using reward and punishment to coerce them into being ethical and efficient. This approach only reveals impatience and a closed mind.

If we are convinced we know everything there is to know about the world, we create a world with little understanding of humanity, where humans are just animals to be controlled and directed. A society thus created, one without faith, is no society at all. It is a warzone waiting to explode.

To understand why people refuse to do as they are told, why they defy and subvert the system, we need Sharda. To get Sharda, the yajaman has to give Vidyalakshmi freely and introspect why the devata resists receiving it, why he would rather obtain fish than learn to fish, why he would rather be dependent and complain about others instead of taking responsibility and becoming dependable.

Ravi compares his mining business to collecting water from a well. When there is a high demand in the market, he widens the bucket and when the demand is low, he narrows it. With this approach of his, he is revealing that he looks at his organization as a mere bucket, a thing. People are just tools to be used as long as they are useful. And then he wonders why, despite being hugely successful, no one in his family looks up to him or cares for him. They fear him, and obey him, but do not appreciate him. He is not in a happy place and will continue to be unhappy if he doesn't widen his gaze to learn and grow.

Growth in thought brings about growth in action

As Vishnu goes about preserving the world, provoking everyone to expand their gaze, we discover how each of his avatars is based on the learning from previous avatars:

- As Matsya, the small fish, who is saved from the big fish by Manu and who saves Manu from pralay, he learns that humanity needs to learn moderation and balance. The helpless cannot be helped at the cost of the environment; the act of feeding must be accompanied by the encouragement to outgrow hunger.
- This leads him to become Kurma or the turtle who upholds the churn that functions only when force is balanced by counter-force, when both parties know when to pull and when to let go. Then he observes the animal nature of man that makes him aggressive, territorial and disrespectful of the boundaries of others.
- In the next avatars of Varaha, the boar, and Narasimha, the man-lion, he uses force to overpower and cunning to control the animal instinct. This does not stop the rise of Bali, who believes that all of life's problems will be solved by distributing wealth. Vishnu learns that humanity needs to expand its gaze from things to thoughts, from Narayani to Narayan.
- So Vaman, the priest, becomes Parashuram, the warrior-priest, who tries to instruct humanity on the value of thoughts over things. When instruction does not work, he becomes Ram, leading by example. But then that leads to pretenders who value rules in letter, not spirit. This leads to the birth of Krishna.

- In the final two avatars, Vishnu breaks the system, almost acting like Shiva, the destroyer, passively withdrawing as a hermit (Shramana, sometimes identified with the Buddha), or actively destroying it like a warlord as Kalki. The point of the destruction is to provoke wisdom.
- With culture gone, nature establishes itself in all its fury. The law of the jungle takes over. The big fish eat the small fish until Manu saves the small fish and reveals that there is still hope for humanity. In this act of saving the fish, humanity displays the first stirrings of dharma, the human potential, motivating Vishnu to renew his cycle once more.

Vyas who put together the Mahabharat and the Purans is described as throwing up his hands in anguish over why people do not follow the dharma that benefits all. Vishnu, on the other hand, is never shown displaying such anguish. The transformation of Brahma is not his key performance indicator. Following dharma is not necessary. It is desirable. If not followed, the organization will collapse, but nature will survive and life will go on. So Vishnu smiles even though Brahma stays petulant.

Birendra believes his father Raghavendra is a successful man because he has made a lot of money. However, for Raghavendra money is not the objective but the outcome of intellectual and emotional growth. He began as a clerk in a small chemical company. He learned new skills and understood how the world worked, gradually becoming more and more successful in every task he undertook. He became an executive, a manager, even a director of his firm before he decided to break free and become an entrepreneur. His learning continued as he decided to mentor more companies as an investor. Before long he became the owner of many industries, but never ceased to learn, observing what made people give their best and what made them insecure. This knowledge made him a better negotiator and dealmaker. He shares his ideas freely and creates opportunities for people to grow, but very few see Saraswati the way he does. Naturally, they are neither as successful nor as content as he is.

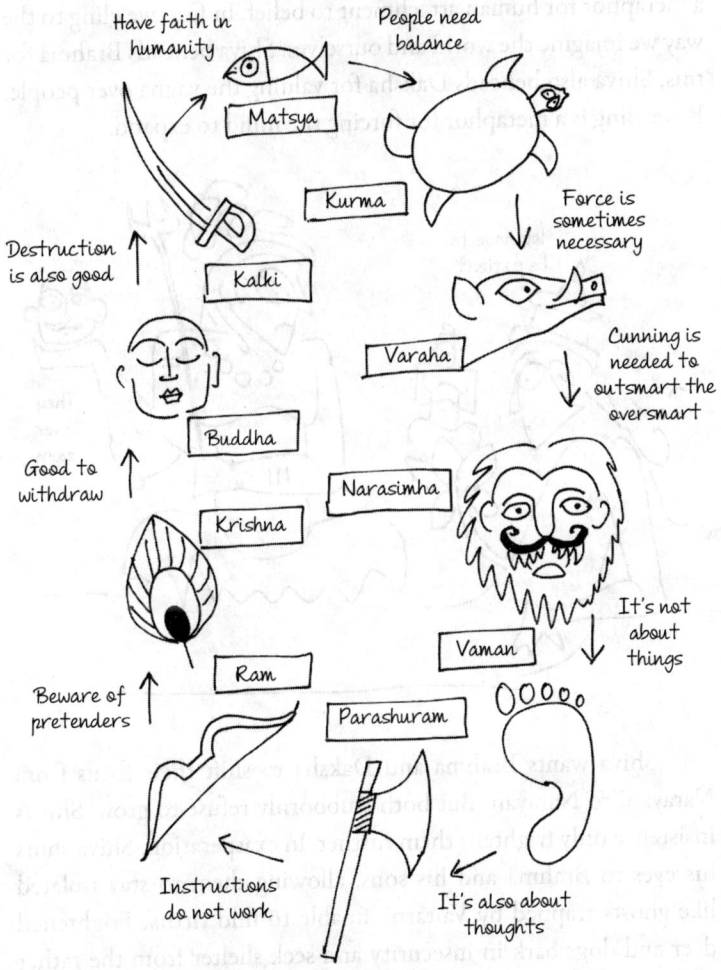

To provoke thought, we have to learn patience

The way Shiva provokes thought is very different from the way Vishnu does. Brahma chases his daughter Shatarupa, which is a metaphor for human attachment to belief. In fear, we cling to the way we imagine the world and ourselves. Shiva beheads Brahma for this. Shiva also beheads Daksha for valuing the yagna over people. Beheading is a metaphor for forcing the mind to expand.

Shiva wants Brahma and Daksha to shift their focus from Narayani to Narayan. But both stubbornly refuse to grow. Shiva's insistence only frightens them further. In exasperation, Shiva shuts his eyes to Brahma and his sons, allowing them to stay isolated like ghosts trapped by Vaitarni, unable to find tirtha. Frightened deer and dogs bark in insecurity and seek shelter from the rather indifferent Shiva.

Shiva is called the destroyer because he rejects Brahma's beliefs, beheads him and holds his skull in his hand in the form of Kapalika. In contrast, Vishnu is called the preserver as he allows Brahma his beliefs, gives him shelter on the lotus that rises from his navel and waits for Brahma to expand his gaze at his own pace and on his own terms.

Vishnu keeps giving the devata the option to change, changing his strategies with each yagna, different avatars for different yugas, sometimes upholding rules, sometimes breaking them, hoping to provoke thought in the devata, to make him do tapasya until shruti is heard.

Like a mother gently persuading her child, Vishnu shows him two things: a wheel (chakra) and a conch shell (shankha). The wheel represents the repetitive nature of prakriti and sanskriti: the changing seasons and the cycle of booms and busts that haunt the marketplace. The conch shell represents the imagination that can spiral outwards in wisdom or inwards in fear.

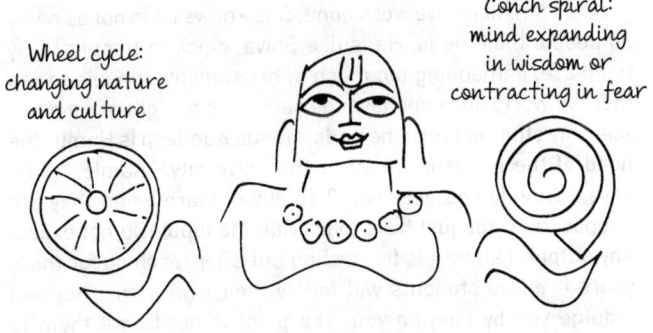

If the devata expands his gaze, the yajaman grows in faith. If the devata does not expand his gaze, the yajaman grows in patience. Either way, the yajaman grows. He sees more, he becomes more inclusive. He does not frighten away investors, talent, or customers who naturally gather around this patient, accommodating being. Thus Lakshmi walks his way.

All her working life, Maria has heard Kamlesh scream, "You will not understand. Just do what I tell you." She has been his secretary for twenty years and she knows that Kamlesh is a brilliant man who wants to share his knowledge with the world, but he has very little patience. As chief designer, he tries hard to explain his designs to his team but they just do not get it. He wins numerous awards and so many designers want to work with him, but while they work with him, few really try and appreciate what makes Kamlesh so brilliant. Kamlesh's thoughts are spatial, not linear. He sees patterns and thinks on his feet, changing ideas constantly, relying very much on instinct. He tries to explain this 'process' but it is very difficult to articulate. When those around him are not able to catch up with him, he loses his temper, shouts at them, calls them names and throws them out. Maria has been able to figure him out enough to know how to work with him. While she does not understand his design work, she knows how to get his administrative work done. She knows he is not as nasty as people think he is. He is like Shiva, quick to temper, easy to please, demanding too much of his students, unable to see that the world does not have the same line of sight as he does. The only other person who understands Kamlesh is Hamir, the head of the art department at the university. "Kamlesh," he says, "Why do you get angry? They will learn when they are supposed to. You just have to provide the input. Do not expect any output. I know it is frustrating but after teaching for thirty years I realize students will follow their own path. They will indulge you by obeying you. The point is not to get them to obey; the point is to inspire them to expand their own mind for their own good. If they don't, who loses?" So saying, Hamir smiles.

Conclusion

Modern management is all about chasing a target, the Promised Land of Abrahamic mythology, Elysium of Greek mythology. Hindu mythology, however, warns against chasing Lakshmi, the goddess of wealth; it will result in conflict. Instead it advises making oneself attractive to Lakshmi, worthy of her affection and auspiciousness, so she walks our way. For that we have to be less like Indra, king of the gods, who is consumed by his own hunger, and more like Vishnu, preserver of the world, who is consumed by other people's hunger. Vishnu knows that human hunger is threefold: for wealth, power and knowledge.

As we have seen, at the heart of the Indian approach to management is the ritual of yagna, the oldest of Hindu rituals mentioned in the very first hymn of the Rig Veda. It is commonly mistranslated as sacrifice, or worship, but in fact means exchange, the cornerstone of any economy. When we give in order to get, we are the yajaman. When we give only after getting, we are the devata. When we seek without giving, we are the asura. When we grab, we are the rakshasa. When we hoard, we are the yaksha. When we do not exchange, we are the shramana, or hermit, who has outgrown his hunger, and so does not seek to be fed, nor feeds. Vishnu is the bhagavan, he who gives despite having outgrown his hunger. He receives only to make the devata feel significant.

The Talent Sutra

The yajaman is a social being: the entrepreneur, the professional, the businessman, the promoter, the manufacturer, the service-provider who satisfies the hunger of a stakeholder, be it customer, employee, vendor, partner, boss or investor, in order to get what he wants. He is always conscious of human hunger, which if not catered to can plunge the world into violence, as we see all around us today.

Modern management has been today reduced to looking at business as a set of targets, or as a set of tasks. But business is essentially about a set of people who satisfy the hunger of the shareholder at one end and consumers at the another. Every stakeholder in business, employees and entrepreneur included, is essentially an animal who can imagine. Like every hungry predator, s/he suffers from the fear of death by starvation, hence seeks food. Like every hunted prey, s/he suffers from the fear of death by predation, hence seeks security and power. This is further fuelled by the imagination, hence creating the insatiable yearning for wealth and power in humans. Further, humans wonder who they are, why they exist, and whether their lives have meaning. This fear of invalidation consumes us. Hence every yajaman needs to have an intimate knowledge of Lakshmi, Durga and Saraswati, the goddesses of wealth, power and knowledge, the hunger for whom exists in different proportions in different stakeholders.

Together the three goddesses (LDS, or LSD, in short) constitute the three arms of human happiness. To make the world a happy place *should be* the ultimate aim of every yagna, hence every business. For this businesses have to be approached as yagnas where we satisfy the other's hunger in order to satisfy ours. That is dharma.

Notes

With new words are created new worlds, as they are vehicles of new ideas. They enable the process of expanding the mind. The words and terms explained below are common to the books in my sutra series—*Business Sutra*, *The Success Sutra*, *The Leadership Sutra* and *The Talent Sutra*.

	Business context	Conventional context
agni	that which is used to tame and control nature	fire god
Amravati	the ideal goal where all needs are met without effort	Indra's paradise
ankush	a tool used for pushing people to do their job, and pulling them back	elephant goad
Arjun	one who argues too much, shooting counter questions like arrows when questioned	the third Pandav who is a skilled archer
asura	one who feels his entitlement has been denied, resulting in rage and ambition	eternal enemies of the devas
avasarpini	pessimistic gaze	waning period of an era
avatar	role adapted to the context for the benefit of the Other	descent of Vishnu
bali	what is destroyed in the process of creation	sacrifice
bhagavan	a being who is not hungry but pays attention to others' hunger	a being who is never hungry but feeds others

	Business context	Conventional context
bhaya	insecurities	fear
Bhim	one who wants to act rather than think	the second Pandav who is very strong
bhog	that which satisfies hunger	consumption
Bhoj	a leader who balances creativity with accountability	a legendary king
Brahma	subject of the subjective truth	the creator
brahmanda	imagined reality	subjective world
chakravarti	the king who controls his kingdom with rules	emperor of the world
Chandra	one who is very moody and has favourites	the moon god
Chaturbhuj	the one who multitasks	another name for Vishnu indicating he has four arms
Chintamani	that which satisfies every wish	wish-fulfilling jewel of paradise
Daksha	one who is obsessed with rules	the patron of the yagna
darshan	observing the subject of subjective reality	gaze
deva	he who sees what comes to him as entitlement	Brahma's sons who live in luxury above the sky
devata	he who responds to the transaction initiated by the yajaman	the deity being invoked
Draupadi	one who has to deal with multiple bosses and subordinates	the common wife of the five Pandavs
drishti	observing objective reality	vision
Durga	power that grants security and authority	goddess of war
dushama	bust	negative period

	Business context	Conventional context
Ganesha	one who can easily wear many hats and so communicate between many departments	the elephant-headed god who removes obstacles
Gangu-teli	the one doing a monotonous job	legendary oil presser
garud-drishti	strategy, wide vision, long-term thinking	bird's-eye view
Gauri	organization based on rules	the domesticated form of the Goddess Kali
Goloka	sustainable happy business	paradise of cows
Gobar-ka-Ganesh	he who does what he is told to do with no view of his own	legendary dumb character
grama-devata	the manager who adapts principles of the centre to the realities of the periphery	village god
Halahal	the negative output of any action	poison that comes with nectar
Hanuman	he who obeys unconditionally and without question	the monkey who serves Ram and is worshipped in his own right
Indra	he who wants high return on investment always	king of devas
ishta-devata	one who grants us personal favours	personal god
Kailas	where there is no hunger	abode of Shiva
Kali	marketplace with no regulatory control	the wild form of the Goddess Gauri
Kalpataru	that which satisfies every wish	wish-fulfilling tree
Kama	right-brain activity, creativity, which does not like structure	god of desire

The Talent Sutra

	Business context	Conventional context
Kamadhenu	that which satisfies every wish	wish-fulfilling cow
karma	consequences of actions	the cycle of cause and consequence
karta	the one who gives the directive	a leader
karya-karta	the one who follows the directive	a follower
Kauravs	those who stubbornly refuse to learn	the hundred brothers led by Duryodhan who oppose the five Pandavs
Krishna	he who breaks rules to help others grow on their terms	cowherd avatar of Vishnu
Kubera	the one who hoards	king of yakshas
kula-devata	one who grants us departmental favours	the family god
Lakshmi	wealth	goddess of wealth
Mitti-ka-Madhav	he who does what he is told to do with no view of his own	folk character
Nakul	one who looks pretty but delivers nothing	the fourth Pandav who is very handsome
Narad	he who makes people insecure by comparing and contrasting	trouble-making sage
Narayan	human potential	God
Narayani	resources	Goddess
nirguna	not measurable	intangible
Pandavs	students who have made mistakes but are open to learning	the five protagonists of the epic Mahabharat
parashu	analysis	axe
Parashuram	leader who punishes rule-breakers sternly	the warrior-sage form of Vishnu

	Business context	Conventional context
pasha	synthesis	string
prakriti	material world	nature
pralay	end of an organization or a market	the end of the world when everything dissolves into the sea
purush	imagination	humanity
Radha	leader who lets talent go without begrudging them	the milkmaid who is the beloved of Krishna
rakshasa	one who takes things by force	demon who grabs
Ram	he who follows the rules at any cost to help others grow on their terms	the royal form of Vishnu
rana-bhoomi	competitive environment	warzone
ranga-boomi	joyful environment where everybody grows	playground
Ravan	he who breaks the rule for his growth at the cost of others	king of rakshasas
rishi	one who has more insight than others	seer who can see what others do not see
saguna	measurable	tangible
Sahadev	one who only speaks when spoken to even though he knows solutions to problems	the youngest Pandav who was very wise and never spoke unless spoken to
sanskriti	culture	society
Saraswati	human imagination	goddess of knowledge
sarpa-drishti	tactic, narrow-vision, short-term thinking	snake vision
sattra	an organization with many processes	a complex set of multiple yagnas
Shakti	inborn strength, capacity and capability	goddess of power

The Talent Sutra

	Business context	Conventional context
Shankar	he who is content and sensitive to others	another name of Shiva
Sharda	knowledge of purusha	goddess of wisdom
Shekchilli	dreamer with no accountability	folk character who dreams
Shiva	he who is independent but withdrawn from the world	God who destroys
shruti	personal ideas that cannot be shared	inner voice that is heard but cannot be spoken or transmitted
smriti	public ideas that are exchanged	outer voice that is spoken or transmitted but not necessarily heard
sthula-sharira	how we appear physically to others	the physical body
Surya	one who is radiant and attracts all attention	the sun god
sushama	boom	positive period
svaha	input	this of me I offer
Swarga	Indra's paradise	another name for Amravati
tapasya	introspection, contemplation, analysis	the practice of churning tapa (mental fire)
tathastu	output	so be it
utasarpini	optimistic gaze	upwards movement of time
Vaikuntha	workplace where everything comes together without conflict	Vishnu's abode in the middle of the ocean of milk
Vaman	he who grows big and thus makes the Other feel small and insignificant	dwarf avatar of Vishnu
vasudev	one who is action driven	the hero who is a man of action who seeks wealth

	Business context	Conventional context
vetal	facilitator who asks questions that provoke thought, but does not know the answer	the teacher who never goes to the student and who provokes discomforting reflections
Vikramaditya	the student who goes to the teacher	a legendary king
Vishnu	he who grows on his terms by enabling others to grow on their terms at their pace	God who preserves
yagna	the process of exchange	Vedic fire ritual
yajaman	the one who initiates the offer of exchange	patron
yaksha	one who hoards	Brahma's son who hoards
Yama	left-brain activity that is highly structured	god of death
yoga	outgrowing hunger	alignment
Yudhishtir	upright but naïve leader	the eldest Pandav

Index of Sutras

The gaze can be cruel or caring *13*

Everyone seeks a caring gaze *16*

We want to be seen as we imagine ourselves *18*

A cruel gaze focuses on our compliance rather than our capability *20*

Unseen, we are compelled to fend for ourselves *22*

We refuse to see ourselves as villains *24*

We use work as a beacon to get attention *27*

Our goals justify our lack of a caring gaze *29*

Fear isolates us while imagination connects us *35*

We often forget that others see the world differently *38*

How we see others reveals who we are *41*

How others see us reveals who we are *44*

The Other reveals the power of our gaze *47*

The Other reveals our insensitivity *49*

The Other reveals our inadequacy *52*

The Other reveals our blindness *54*

Growth happens when the mind expands *59*

Growth is about pursuing thoughts not things *62*

Growth is indicated when we prefer giving than taking *65*

Growth happens when more people can depend on us *68*

Growth happens when even the insignificant become significant *70*

Growth happens when we include those whom we once excluded *72*

Growth happens when we stop seeing people as villains *74*

Growth happens when we seek to uplift the Other *76*

More yajamans are needed as an organization grows *81*

The yajaman has to turn devatas into yajamans *83*

Creating talent enables us to grow *85*

We seek to inherit things, not thoughts *87*

Being a yajaman is about gaze, not skills *89*

Questions teach us, not answers *91*

We resist advice and instructions *94*

Discourses never transform us *96*

Crisis increases the chances of learning *98*

Power play underlies the process of teaching *101*

To teach, we have to learn to let go *103*

Only when teachers are willing to learn does growth happen *105*

Growth in thought brings about growth in action *107*

To provoke thought, we have to learn patience *110*

ALSO BY DEVDUTT PATTANAIK
BUSINESS SUTRA
A Very Indian Approach to Management

In this landmark book, bestselling author, leadership coach and mythologist Devdutt Pattanaik shows how, despite its veneer of objectivity, modern management is rooted in Western beliefs and obsessed with accomplishing rigid objectives and increasing shareholder value. By contrast, the Indian way of doing business—as apparent in Indian mythology, but no longer seen in practice—accommodates subjectivity and diversity, and offers an inclusive, more empathetic way of achieving success. Great value is placed on darshan, that is, on how we see the world and our relationship with Lakshmi, the goddess of wealth.

Business Sutra uses stories, symbols and rituals drawn from Hindu, Jain and Buddhist mythology to understand a wide variety of business situations that range from running a successful tea stall to nurturing talent in a large multinational corporation. At the heart of the book is a compelling premise: if we believe that wealth needs to be chased, the workplace becomes a rana-bhoomi—a battleground of investors, regulators, employers, employees, vendors, competitors and customers; if we believe that wealth needs to be attracted, the workplace becomes a ranga-bhoomi—a playground where everyone is happy.

Brilliantly argued, original and thoroughly accessible, *Business Sutra* presents a radical and nuanced approach to management, business and leadership in a diverse, fast-changing, and increasingly polarized world.

THE SUCCESS SUTRA
An Indian Approach to Wealth

Most human beings hunger after riches and success. There are any number of management books which provide theories and techniques on how to become rich and successful. All of them advise us to chase Lakshmi, the goddess of wealth, in order to make her our own. But the Indian approach to prosperity and fulfilment warns against the relentless pursuit of the goddess, writes noted thinker and mythologist Devdutt Pattanaik, as it will result in conflict. Rather, we have to give in order to get, we have to satisfy the hunger of others in order to satisfy our own. If we learn and practise this fundamental truth, Lakshmi will enter our homes and our lives.

Derived from his acclaimed bestseller *Business Sutra*, this book is filled with lessons and insights into management, business and the creation of wealth and success.

THE LEADERSHIP SUTRA
An Indian Approach to Power

Durga is the goddess of power in Hinduism, as well as in Buddhism and Jainism. Her name is derived from the word 'fortress' (durg). She is the goddess of kings. She rides a lion, the king of the jungle and a symbol of royalty everywhere from China to England. We tend to tiptoe around the role of power in management, and fail to openly acknowledge how the animal desire to dominate often destroys the best of organizations. Critics tend to see power as a negative thing. But power is a critical tool that affects the implementation of any idea. Any attempt to restrain it with rules results in domestication and resentment, and fails to energize the organization. Leaders often equate themselves with lions, and indulge their desire to dominate when, in fact, the point of leadership is to be secure enough to outgrow the lion within us, and enable and empower those around us. But this is not easy, as anxiety overpowers the best of leaders.

Derived from Devdutt Pattanaik's influential bestseller *Business Sutra*, this book offers startling and original insights into the exercise of power and leadership. It explores the human quest for significance, the power of rules to rob people of self-esteem, and the need for stability even at the cost of freedom.